LEICESTER & RUTLAND

PAST

A GUIDE TO HISTORIC PLACES AND PEOPLE

DAVID GERRARD

ALAN SUTTON PUBLISHING LIMITED

First published in the United Kingdom in 1996
Alan Sutton Publishing Limited · Phoenix Mill · Far Thrupp · Stroud
Gloucestershire

British Library Cataloguing in Publication Data

A catalogue record for this book is available from the British Library

ISBN 0-7509-1039-9

Typeset in 9/13 Sabon.
Typesetting and origination by
Alan Sutton Publishing Limited.
Printed in Great Britain by
Hartnolls, Bodmin, Cornwall

CONTENTS

Melton Mowbray

INTRODUCTION

At Braunston, a voluptuously plump pagan goddess leans against the outside wall of the village church, a symbol of fertility whose gap-eyed gaze looks coldly across the ranks of Christian dead. In Bradgate Park near Leicester, atop one of the loftiest hills in these low-lying counties, stands a curious structure resembling nothing so much as a huge stone tankard – a folly raised by an indulgent master in memory of an unfortunate servant. At Clipsham, flanking a broad grassy avenue, stretch two 700-yd lines of sculpted trees: an elephant looks across to a ballerina, a Spitfire takes off towards a battleship and Diddy-men cavort near a windmill in an extraordinary treasury of topiary begun more than 120 years ago. These, and more than a hundred other relics of Leicestershire and Rutland's past, are included in this book. Many of them cast a curious light on the social customs of our ancestors, such as the finger pillory in Ashby de la Zouch church, a bizarre form of ecclesiastical punishment. Or Sir Joseph Danvers' 'half-sacred, half-profane' tomb in Swithland churchyard: the portion within consecrated ground preserves the remains of Sir Joseph himself, the unblessed part beyond the graveyard boundary contains those of his favourite dog.

Some are hidden away in village byways (such as Topsy Turvey's gibbet near Bilstone); others in busy cities are passed unnoticed by thousands every day, such as Arthur Wakerley's exuberant building, the Turkey Café, in Leicester's Granby Street. The vast majority of them are easily accessible although the current, sadly necessary, practice of locking churches during most of the week may require you to seek out the vicar or churchwarden. Occasionally, a familiar name crops up in an unexpected context – King Richard III, for example. At Donington le Heath you can see the bed in which he slept the night before the Battle of Bosworth. And at Market Overton, the old stocks and whipping post that stand on the green would be recognized by Isaac Newton who lived in the village as a boy. Then there are rather less well known figures. Percy Pilcher was one of the pioneers of powered flight: the extraordinary apparatus in which he made his last, fatal flight can be seen at Stanford Hall. In Oakham, the house of 'Tom Thumb' still stands. Barely 33 inches tall, Jeffery Hudson was 'baked in a pie' for Charles I, whose Queen, Henrietta, was so taken by the novelty she carried him off to court.

Although I have lived in Leicestershire for some years, a good number of the subjects in this book were new discoveries. I hope readers will be as intrigued and surprised by them as much as I have been myself.

David Gerrard

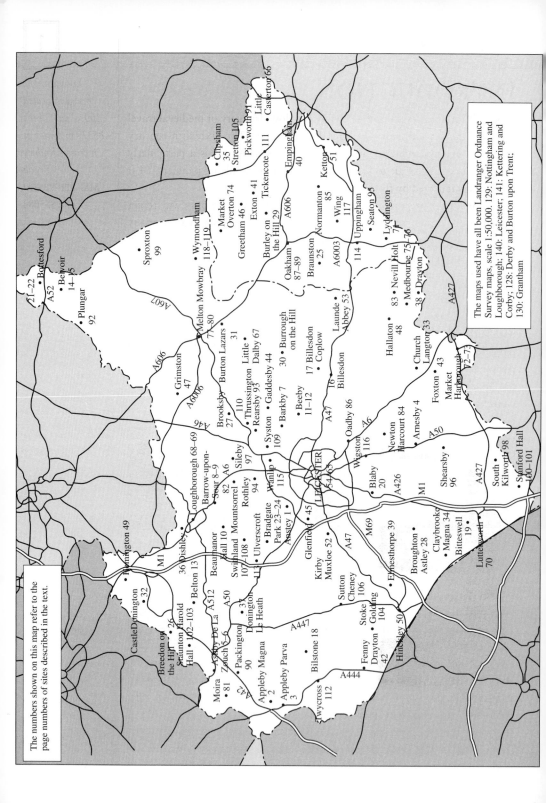

The numbers shown on this map refer to the page numbers of sites described in the text.

The maps used have all been Landranger Ordnance Survey maps, scale 1:50,000. 129: Nottingham and Loughborough; 140: Leicester; 141: Kettering and Corby; 128: Derby and Burton upon Trent; 130: Grantham.

Bottesford 21–22
Belvoir 14–15
Plungar 92
Sproxton 99
Clipsham 35
Stretton 105
Pickworth 91
Little Casterton 66
Empingham 40
Wymondham 118–119
Market Overton 74
Exton 41
Tickencote 111
Ketton 51
Greetham 46
Burley on the Hill 29
Normanton 85
Wing 117
Melton Mowbray 77–80
Oakham 87–89
A606
Braunston 25
Seaton 95
Uppingham 71
Lyddington 71
Grimston 47
Burton Lazars
Little Dalby 67
Burrough on the Hill 30
Billesdon 17
Coplow
Launde Abbey 53
Nevill Holt 83
Medbourne 75–76
Drayton 38
Brooksby 27
Thrussington 110
Rearsby 93
Gaddesby 44
Beeby 11–12
Hallaton 48
Church Langton 33
Foxton 43
Market Harborough 72–73
Loughborough 68–69
Barrow-upon-Soar 8–9
Sileby 97
Syston 109
Barkby 7
Billesdon
Oadby 86
Newton Harcourt 84
Arnesby 4
Lockington 49
Beaumanor Hall 10
Swithland 107–108
Mountsorrel
Rothley 94
Ulverscroft 113
Bradgate Park 23–24
Astley 1
Wanlip 115
Glenfield 45
LEICESTER 54–65
Wigston 116
Blaby 20
Shearsby 96
South Kilworth 98
Stanford Hall 100–101
Castle Donington 32
Breedon on the Hill 26
Staunton Harold Hall 102–103
Belton 13
Ashby De La Zouch 5–6
Packington 90
Donington Le Heath 37
Kirby Muxloe 52
Sutton Cheney 106
Earl Shilton 39
Claybrooke Magna 34
Bitteswell 19
Lutterworth 70
Moira 81
Appleby Magna 2
Appleby Parva 3
Bilstone 18
Fenny Drayton 42
Stoke Golding 104
Hinckley 50
Twycross 112

ANSTEY

Ned Ludd's Bridge

Location: The bridge is located 100 yd west of the B5327 in Anstey as it crosses Rothley Brook

MAP REFERENCE: 140: 553084

Nothing conjures up so vividly the slow drudgery of medieval travel as a well-preserved pack-horse bridge. The sixteenth-century example which crosses Rothley Brook at Anstey is a particularly fine specimen: 5 ft wide to give space for the horse's bulging panniers, 54 ft long and supported by five low arches.

In the late eighteenth century, when the bridge was the only way to get to Leicester, some four miles distant, it would have been crossed many times by Ned Ludd (or Ludlam). Ned was born in Anstey around 1760 and is routinely described in histories of the period as 'half-witted', a 'lunatic' or 'simpleton'. His 'idiotic' view was that the new mechanical stocking-frames were reducing the village's home-knitters to penury and his response was to set fire to these baleful harbingers of the Industrial Revolution. The 'Luddite' movement gained strength across the Midlands until in 1818 the Government swooped on six of its leaders and hanged them all at Nottingham; no more was heard of Ned Ludd's seditious ideas.

OTHER PLACES OF INTEREST

There's a second, later, pack-horse bridge at Anstey in Sheepwash Lane; Bradgate Park (p. 24) to the north-west; Rothley (p. 94) and Wanlip (p.115) to the north; Leicester (p. 54) to the south.

APPLEBY MAGNA

*Location: Appleby
Magna lies on the
western edge of the
county, 7 miles
south-west of Ashby
de la Zouch, 1 mile
south of Junction 11
of the M42*
MAP REFERENCE:
128: 317097

A Moat without a Manor

I t's one of the most picturesque groupings to be seen in Leicestershire – a sturdy fifteenth-century gatehouse to a now-vanished manor house with, nestling alongside, a lovely timber-framed cottage built a hundred years later (and still occupied).

Around them on three sides runs the moat that provided an extra defence for the stone-built house that William de Appleby erected here in 1166. Sadly, that's all that's known about him so we have no idea how he acquired the funds to build in such an expensive material. Nor do we know which of his descendants was rich enough to put up such a 'monumental and forbidding' gatehouse, as Pevsner calls it.

*OTHER PLACES
OF INTEREST*

*Moira (p. 81) to the
north; Appleby
Parva (next page) to
the south.*

APPLEBY PARVA

The Grandest Primary School in England

B y any standards, the Church of England primary school in Appleby Parva is a remarkable building. Three storeys high, with a five-arched entrance and topped by an elegant cupola, it's one of the most impressive structures to be seen in west Leicestershire.

It was built towards the end of the 1600s as a Grammar School by Sir John Moore who lived at nearby Appleby Hall (now demolished). Sir John, Lord Mayor of London in 1697, had made a sizeable fortune from the East India spice trade and when he decided to build a boarding school for the 'sons of gentlemen of the county' he consulted his friend Sir Christopher Wren. Wren was too busy to undertake the work himself but recommended a disciple, Sir William Wilson, whose designs he scrutinized and approved.

Seventy years later, Dr Samuel Johnson applied for the post of headmaster here. Fortunately for English literature he was not appointed. After being unoccupied for many years, the building was re-opened in the 1950s and must, by a long way, be the grandest primary school in England.

Location: Appleby Parva is on the A444, about 1 mile south of Junction 1 of the M42. The school is on an unclassified road leading from the centre of the village to Appleby Magna
MAP REFERENCE:
128: 314092

OTHER PLACES OF INTEREST

Appleby Magna (p. 2) and Moira (p. 81) to the north; Bilstone (p. 18) to the south-east.

ARNESBY

A Rare Survival

Location: Arnesby
is just west of the
A50 Leicester–
Northampton road,
about 12 miles
south of Leicester.
The windmill stands
just north of the
village
MAP REFERENCE:
140: 615925

Very few windmills have survived in Leicestershire and Rutland and none of them is in working order. The fine example at Arnesby was built in 1815 replacing an earlier post-mill erected in 1653.

The present mill continued working until 1914 but was then left to decay until 1976 when it was restored to its original external appearance, and a house was built alongside. It stands in private grounds but is easily visible from the road and from a public footpath that passes nearby.

*OTHER PLACES
OF INTEREST*

*Leicester (p. 54),
Oadby (p. 86) and
Wigston (p. 116) to
the north; Market
Harborough (p. 72)
to the south-east;
Stanford Hall
(p. 100) to the
south-west;
Lutterworth (p. 70)
to the west.*

Ashby de la Zouch

Ivanhoe's Romantic Castle

Location: Ashby de
la Zouch is on the
western edge of the
county, where the
A50 and A453
cross. Signposted
from the M42 at
Junction 13
MAP REFERENCE:
128: 361168

We've become accustomed to seeing tourist-hungry councils packaging swathes of the country and naming them after popular television series: 'Herriot Country' in the Yorkshire Dales, 'Poldark Country' in Cornwall, 'Catherine Cookson Country' in the north east. There's nothing new about the practice – Ashby de la Zouch was promoting itself as 'Ivanhoe Country' soon after Sir Walter Scott's novel, set in and around Ashby Castle, was published in 1820. Visitors came to admire the stately ruins of the castle and to stroll across the tournament field where Ivanhoe jousted so successfully in defence of his lady-love.

Originally a Norman manor house, it was converted into a massive fortress by Lord Hastings in the fifteenth century. Visitors can still climb the magnificent Hastings Tower which was completed in 1464 and can also explore the underground passage that connects it to the kitchens. During the Civil War it was besieged for more than a year by the Parliamentary forces and, following their victory, partly destroyed. It remained neglected until Sir Walter's romantic tale stirred public interest in the grand old building.

OTHER PLACES
OF INTEREST

St Helen's Church,
Ashby (next page);
Staunton Harold
(p. 102) to the
north; Breedon on
the Hill (p. 26) to
the north-east;
Moira (p. 81) to the
south-west.

ASHBY DE LA ZOUCH

*Location: Ashby de
la Zouch is on the
western edge of the
county, where the
A50 and A453
cross. Signposted
from the M42 at
Junction 13*
MAP REFERENCE:
128: 361168

A Pillory for Fingers

This attractive little town offers many diversions to its visitors but one of the most unorthodox is a barbarous little instrument constructed of mellowed oak standing at the west end of St Helen's Church. It's a finger pillory, the only one in Britain. The two beams each have thirteen hollowed grooves (to fit fingers and hand-spans of all sizes) between which the offender's digits were clamped. History doesn't record which particular misdemeanours during Divine Service merited such a curious punishment.

More conventional attractions in the church include some fine tombs, Rysbrack's tenderly sculpted head of the Countess of Huntingdon, and a series of stained glass windows depicting the life of Christ which are reckoned to be the finest in the Midlands.

*OTHER PLACES
OF INTEREST*

*Ashby Castle
(previous page);
Staunton Harold
(p. 102) to the
north; Breedon on
the Hill (p. 26) to
the north-east;
Moira (p. 81) to the
south-west.*

BARKBY

The 'Moody Bush' Stone

7

Location: From the
roundabout on the
A607 at
Queniborough, take
the first left, an
unclassified road
signposted to
Barkby. The stone is
in a field on the left
about 2 miles down
this road
MAP REFERENCE:
129: 637105

No one knows who put the old stone there. Bearing just the two words 'Moody Bush', it stands in the corner of a field adjoining The Ridgemere, a Bronze Age track between Barkby and Syston. The most plausible explanation is that the stone commemorates the first meeting of the East Goscote Hundreds Court held on Moody Bush Hill in 1346. These Courts were frequently held in the open air if there was no building large enough to accommodate all those entitled to take part and were known then as 'Moots' from the old Norse word for a meeting.

Hence the 'Mooty Bush', later corrupted into 'Moody Bush'. The Court assembled at least twice a year and all freeholders were required to be present. Their responsibilities included the apprehension and punishment of malefactors as well as the general good government of the Hundreds. In many respects, they were the forerunners of the parish and borough councils of later years.

OTHER PLACES
OF INTEREST

Gaddesby (p. 44) to
the north-west;
Beeby (p. 11) to
the south-east;
Leicester (p. 54) to
the south-west.

BARROW UPON SOAR

Location: In the
centre of Barrow,
just to the east of
the B675
MAP REFERENCE:
129: 576177

At the Sign of the Plesiosaurus

The people of Barrow upon Soar seem to have a taste for the unusual – where else would you find beneath the name-plate as you enter the village a sculpted plesiosaurus? A fossilized sea-reptile of this kind was unearthed here in 1851 while the foundations for a villa were being excavated.

More eccentricity is to be found in the church. In these days, a family's wish to put 'Gran' or 'Dad' on a gravestone can see them ending up as defendants in an ecclesiastical court. So it's refreshing to find that Barrow's seventeenth-century parson took a more robust and tolerant view of what is acceptable as an epitaph. A tablet in Holy Trinity Church records the death in 1656 of Theophilus Cave with a jokey, punning inscription:

> Here in this grave there lyes a Cave,
> We call a Cave a Grave,
> If Cave be Grave and Grave be Cave,
> Then reader judge I crave
> Whether doth Cave lye in Grave
> Or Grave here lye in Cave?
> If Grave in Cave here buried lye
> Then Grave where is thy victorie?
> Goe reader and report here lyes a Cave
> Who conquers death and buries his own Grave.

Another curiosity in the village is an eighteenth-century wooden board bearing the warning: 'All Vagrants who are found Begging in this town will be taken up and PROSECUTED'.

OTHER PLACES
OF INTEREST

Sileby (p. 97) to the
south-east;
Mountsorrel (p. 82)
to the south;
Loughborough
(p. 68) to the
north-west.

BARROW UPON SOAR

'Cave Bibles' for the Children

Location: In the
centre of Barrow,
just to the east of
the B675
MAP REFERENCE:
129: 576177

Theophilus Cave is remembered in Barrow upon Soar not just for his punning epitaph (*see opposite*) but also for the various bequests left by his nephew, Humphrey Babington, in memory of his uncle. One of them provided funds for the children of the parish to be presented with 'Cave Bibles' – a bequest that is still honoured annually. Humphrey also founded 'The Old Men's Hospital', a charming building in brick and stone that stands just across from the church. The 'Bedesmen' were provided with shelter, fuel and money, and given blue and cream robes which they donned each Sunday to process to the church. They entered by their very own door and then took their special seats in the chancel, a custom which continued from the founding of the Hospital in 1694 until 1938.

There were conditions. The Bedesmen were required to be inside by 7 o'clock in the evening for supper. They had to attend prayers at 8 o'clock and the doors were closed at 9 o'clock. Riotous or disorderly conduct was punished by expulsion. The Hospital is currently a Trust providing flats for the elderly, and women too are now eligible. Two large boards in Holy Trinity Church give full details of the foundation.

OTHER PLACES
OF INTEREST

Sileby (p. 97) to the
south-east;
Mountsorrel (p. 82)
to the south;
Loughborough
(p. 68) to the north-
west.

BEAUMANOR HALL

A Riot of Heraldry

*Location: In
Woodhouse village,
just west of the
B591.*
MAP REFERENCE:
129: 537156

Perhaps the most impressive stained glass window in Leicestershire is to be found not in any of the county's churches but at Beaumanor Hall, the seat of the Herrick family from 1595 to the 1930s. The present Tudor-style mansion was built in 1848 and it was then that the extraordinary window, 15 ft wide and 25 ft high, was installed by William Perry Herrick. It provides a dramatic greeting for visitors entering the lofty reception hall.

All his life William was obsessed with his family pedigree and each of the twenty-one panels in the great window features the brilliantly coloured coat-of-arms of one of his ancestors. It's a breath-taking riot of heraldry, making splendid use of the newly discovered art of producing 'medieval' stained glass. Sadly, for a man who took such pride in his ancestry, William was to die without a direct heir to succeed him.

Beaumanor Hall is now a Leicestershire County Council training centre but the window may be viewed by prior arrangement by calling (01509) 890119.

*OTHER PLACES
OF INTEREST*

*Loughborough
(p. 68) to the north;
Mountsorrel (p. 82)
to the east;
Swithland (p. 107)
to the south.*

BEEBY

An Unfortunate Church

11

*Location: Beeby is
on an unclassified
road between
Barkby and South
Croxton about
6 miles north-east of
Leicester*
MAP REFERENCE:
141: 664084

'Ridiculous', 'unfortunate', 'grotesque' – no one seems to have a kind word for the truncated spire atop All Saints' Church in Beeby. Money was clearly running out even before the builders started on the spire for the lower part of the tower is faced with expensive ashlar, but higher up this gives way to more economical ironstone. There was then to have been a traditional, graceful Leicestershire spire but, when funds finally dried up, the work was abandoned leaving a squat, octagonal stump – 'The Tub' or 'Coffee Pot' as it's known locally. A more colourful legend asserts that the spire was left unfinished because the chief mason, finding that he couldn't match the height of Queniborough church spire nearby, threw himself off Beeby tower in a fit of professional pique.

An even more grisly variation of the tale says that the two masons working at Beeby had themselves built Queniborough's soaring spire and were intending to match it. However, they fell out when one of them asserted that Beeby's tower could not bear such weight. While standing on the tower, their quarrel escalated into a physical struggle during which they both fell to their deaths.

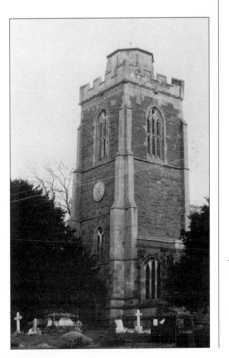

*OTHER PLACES
OF INTEREST*

*Gaddesby (p. 44) to
the north; Leicester
(p. 54) to the south-
west; Barkby (p. 7)
to the north-west.*

BEEBY

*Location: Beeby is
on an unclassified
road between
Barkby and South
Croxton about 6
miles north-east of
Leicester*
MAP REFERENCE:
141: 663083

The Rhyming Well

The Holy Well in Beeby, also known as the Stockwell, was the focal point of the village for centuries. Its unfailing flow of 'excellent mineral waters' serviced not only the people of Beeby but also the village brewery. An illustration in Nichols' *History and Antiquities of Leicestershire*, published in 1815, shows the well protected by a small stone structure with a pitched roof.

In 1855 the villagers clubbed together and built a more imposing, 5 ft high truncated pyramid above it. A plaque was attached celebrating the well's virtues:

> In summer's heat and winter's cold
> One constant temperature I hold
> When brooks and wells and rivers dry
> I always yield a full supply.
> My neighbours say (I'm often told)
> I'm more than worth my weight in gold.

By the mid-twentieth century, this inscription had become badly weatherworn so, as part of the village's Coronation commemoration in 1953, a new plaque was provided. Sadly, under current regulations, the well's water is no longer classified as potable.

*OTHER PLACES
OF INTEREST*

*Gaddesby (p. 44) to
the north; Leicester
(p. 54) to the south-
west; Barkby (p. 7)
to the north-west.*

BELTON

A Living Tradition

Location: Belton
village lies just
north of the B5234
in the north-west
corner of the county
MAP REFERENCE:
129: 448208

Afew Leicestershire villages still celebrate May Day with dancing round a maypole but Belton is unique not only in continuing the old tradition but also in having a maypole standing permanently in the centre of the village. This lofty pole, topped by a weather vane in the form of a fox, is painted in patriotic red, white and blue. Each May Day the dancing is followed by the crowning of the May Queen, a ritual that some antiquarians believe has its roots in pagan fertility ceremonies with the maypole as a phallic symbol.

The village guide book records that on one occasion the pole was 'stolen under cover of darkness by a band of Shepshed marauders, the two villages always having been poles apart (forgive the pun). The intention was to erect it in their own village. But someone raised the alarm and enraged Beltonians pursued the raiders, gave battle and were victorious'. In a separate incident, the pole was knocked down by a reversing bus.

OTHER PLACES
OF INTEREST

Castle Donington
(p. 32) to the north;
Dishley (p. 36) to
the east; Breedon on
the Hill (p. 26) to
the north-west.

BELVOIR CASTLE

*Location: The
Castle is signposted
from the A52
Nottingham–
Grantham road,
and from the A607
Grantham–Melton
Mowbray road*
MAP REFERENCE:
130: 820337

A Fairy Tale Castle

Belvoir Castle (pronounce it *Beever Cassle* if you're asking for directions) is perhaps the most dramatically sited inland castle in England. A huge ridge rises from the Vale of Belvoir and there, perched on its most westerly edge, looms a fairy tale castle. From its topmost towers, the nineteenth-century Dukes of Rutland could look across lands in three counties and know that they owned most of what they saw.

There's been a castle here ever since William the Conqueror's liege-man Robert de Todeni, in the late eleventh century, recognized the value of its strategic setting. The present building, though, is a romantic early nineteenth-century recreation by the architect James Wyatt of an 'ideal' medieval castle, and it's none the worse for that. White's Directory in 1846 described it as 'by far the most superb architectural ornament of which Leicestershire can boast'.

Opening times. 2 April – 29 September: 11.00 a.m. – 5.00 p.m. (Tuesday, Wednesday, Thursday & Saturday); 11.00 a.m. – 6.00 p.m. (Sunday, Good Friday & Bank Holidays). October: 11.00 a.m. – 5.00 p.m. (Sunday). Tel: (01476) 870262.

*OTHER PLACES
OF INTEREST*

*Bottesford (p. 21) to
the north; Plungar
(p. 92) to the east.*

BELVOIR CASTLE

The Belvoir Castle Railway

One of the earliest railways in the country was built in 1793 by the Duke of Rutland. Three miles long, it extended from the Grantham Canal to the Duke's family seat at Belvoir Castle. For more than a hundred years, the line was in daily use with horses drawing wagon-loads of coal from the canal wharf and up the steep hill on which the castle sits.

Short stretches of the old track can still be seen in the Castle grounds. The rails were built to Mr William Jessop's revolutionary new design. Until 1789 rails had always had a flange to keep the wheels from slipping off – William Jessop's bright idea was to put the flange on the wheel and keep the rails flat, an innovation that became standard across the world.

Location: The Castle is signposted from the A52 Nottingham–Grantham road, and from the A607 Grantham–Melton Mowbray road
MAP REFERENCE:
130: 820337

OTHER PLACES
OF INTEREST

Bottesford (p. 21) to the north; Plungar (p. 92) to the east.

BILLESDON

A Distinguished Village School

Despite its minuscule size, the school at Billesdon enjoyed a formidable reputation during the early seventeenth century. It was run by the vicar, the Revd Anthony Cade, who died in 1638 at the early age of 39 but was long remembered for the quality of his teaching. Amongst his pupils were George Fox, founder of the Quakers, and George Villiers from nearby Brooksby Hall. Villiers later became a favourite of James I and was eventually made Duke of Buckingham (*see also* Brooksby, p. 27) but his arrogance and unpopular policies led to his assassination. One of the Duke's biographers records that Villiers was a pupil of Cade until the age of 13 and was 'taught the principles of music and other slight literature'.

The building near the church known as The Old School was probably built a few years after these distinguished alumni had moved on. Probably erected about 1650 using local ironstone, it has a sundial at each end and was originally thatched.

OTHER PLACES OF INTEREST

Launde (p. 53) to the east; Hallaton (p. 48) to the south-east; Church Langton (p. 33) to the south; Leicester (p. 54) to the west.

BILLESDON COPLOW

Captain Becher's Memorable Race

Location: Billesdon
village is just off the
A47, about 8 miles
east of Leicester.
Billesdon Coplow is
about 1.2 miles
north of the village
along an unclassi-
fied road
MAP REFERENCE:
141: 710045

In Old English the word 'Coplow' meant 'a summit and mound', probably a burial mound. Close to Billesdon Coplow rise two hills, Whatborough and Robin a Tiptoe, whose softly rounded contours led one writer to describe them as 'the motherly bosom of Leicestershire'. Billesdon Coplow was the destination for riders in the first 'marked-out' cross-country contest in England, held in 1829. The race began at Noseley and was won by Mr Field Nicholson on Sir Harry Goodricke's 'Magic'. Amongst the unplaced riders was Captain Becher, known as the 'Father of Gentlemen Riders'; his name was later immortalized by his connection with the Aintree Grand National and the famous brook there that was named after him.

OTHER PLACES
OF INTEREST

Launde (p. 53) to
the east; Hallaton
(p. 48) to the south-
east; Church
Langton (p. 33) to
the south; Leicester
(p. 54) to the west.

BILSTONE

Location: Turn left
off the A444, about
2 miles south of
Twycross. The
gibbet is about
2 miles along this
unclassified road,
on the right hand
side
MAP REFERENCE:
140: 362045

'Topsy Turvey's Gibbet'

John Massey seems to have been a singularly unlikeable man. Powerfully built, he had been a successful wrestler in his youth, attracting the nickname 'Topsy Turvey' for the frequency with which he threw opponents over his head. But this enormously strong man was also 'much addicted to passion', and in March 1801, following an argument with his wife, he kicked her into the mill-stream at Bilstone. Massey compounded his crime by then throwing his ten-year-old daughter, the only witness, into the water also. She survived and her testimony ensured Massey's conviction and subsequent execution at Red Hill, Birstall.

The judge had ordered that Massey's body be hung in chains and a gibbet was set up on Congerstone Heath within sight of the pool where the dastardly deed had been committed. J. Potter Briscoe visited the site in 1818: 'At that time, most of the bones were in a tolerable state of preservation, but the flesh and entrails had entirely disappeared. Here and there on the skeleton portions of his clothes still remained'. By the end of the nineteenth century, no traces remained and the gibbet post lay in a ditch. The gibbet was later re-erected by Earl Howe of nearby Gopsall Park and a plaque attached which incorrectly placed the murder in February 1800, thirteen months before it actually happened. That plaque too has disappeared and only the gaunt weathered stump now remains.

OTHER PLACES
OF INTEREST

King Dick's Well,
Sutton Cheney
(p. 106) to the
south-east; Stoke
Golding (p. 104)
and Fenny Drayton
(p. 42) to the south;
Appleby Magna
(p. 2) and Appleby
Parva (p. 3) to the
north-west.

BITTESWELL

Memorial to a Tea Magnate

Location: On the B577, 1.5 miles north of Lutterworth, near the Warwickshire border and the M1/M69 junction
MAP REFERENCE: 140: 537858

In the churchyard of St Mary's stands a memorial of a kind fairly common in the south east of England but unusual, even rare, in the Midlands. It's a wooden graveboard – a horizontal board about a foot above the ground and supported by two Celtic crosses. The monument records the death of Richard Twining at the age of 99 in 1906. Richard was a member of the 'Twining's Tea' family, 'suppliers of tea to the nobility and gentry'. Their history stretches back to 1706 when Thomas Twining established his tea and coffee shop in Temple Bar, London, and the ninth generation of the family is running the business today.

Richard retired to Bitteswell where his sister Mary was married to the Revd James Powell, vicar of the parish, a union that endured for fifty-five years. It was in memory of the vicar that Richard Twining presented the church lych-gate and later gave a plot of land for the cemetery on Ullesthorpe Road.

OTHER PLACES OF INTEREST

Broughton Astley (p. 28) to the north; Stanford Hall (p. 100) and Lutterworth (p. 70) to the south-east; Hinckley (p. 50) to the north-west.

BLABY

Location: Blaby is
4 miles south of
Leicester, just east
of the A426 road to
Lutterworth
MAP REFERENCE:
140: 570979

'Jump when the Bell Rings!'

It seems to have been quite a common practice in the late eighteenth century for persons of substance to have their church memorials firmly in place long before they actually departed this vale of tears. One such was the Revd Edward Stokes (1706–98), rector of All Saints', Blaby, for fifty years. On the attractive gold- and blue-painted tablet to his family he added his own name 'to save trouble, and preserve the uniformity of the stone'. Economizing on such details as the dates of their decease, the monument fuzzily records that the family members were all interred there 'in the eighteenth century' – something the Revd Edward only just achieved, dying in 1798.

A more remarkable fact about Edward Stokes is that although he was blinded in a shooting accident at the age of 8, he became an active and vigorous pastor, relying upon others only for the reading of the lessons. And in the best tradition of eighteenth-century 'squarsons' he was an enthusiastic huntsman. A companion riding alongside would ring a bell when a hedge or ditch needed to be jumped. It sounds like a recipe for disaster but clearly it worked – the rector died quietly in his bed at the age of 92.

*OTHER PLACES
OF INTEREST*

Leicester (p. 54) to
the north;
Broughton Astley
(p. 28) to the south;
Elmesthorpe (p. 39)
to the north-west.

BOTTESFORD

'Wicked Practice and Sorcery'

21

Location:
Bottesford is 8 miles
west of Grantham,
just off the A52.
The church, with its
150 ft spire, is easily
discovered
MAP REFERENCE:
130: 807392

The chancel of St Mary's Church, Bottesford, is truly quite astonishing. Only in Westminster Abbey is there anything to compare with this lavish collection of grandiose but touching monuments to the Earls of Rutland who lived at Belvoir Castle nearby. Filial duty had clearly dictated that heirs should spare no expense in commemorating their sixteenth- and seventeenth-century fathers, Lords of the Vale of Belvoir. By the eighteenth century, there was no room left in the chancel: later Earls and Dukes were interred in an austere mausoleum at the Castle itself.

The most imposing of the Bottesford monuments, which records the death of the 6th Earl in 1632, is also the only one in England that refers to the ghastly witch-hunts of the early seventeenth century. Two of the Earl's children had died unexpectedly. Three unpopular local women, after a farcical trial, were convicted of bringing about the children's deaths by 'wicked practice and sorcery', and were executed. The sorry tale casts a sombre light over one of the grandest memorials in the country.

OTHER PLACES
OF INTEREST

Belvoir Castle
(p. 14) and Plungar
(p. 92) to the south-
west, and see
following page.

22

BOTTESFORD

A Gruesome Gathering of Gargoyles

Location:
Bottesford is 8 miles
west of Grantham,
just off the A52.
The church, with its
150 ft spire, is easily
discovered
MAP REFERENCE:
130: 807392

In addition to its sumptuous collection of monuments to the Earls of Rutland (*see previous page*), Bottesford Church is remarkable for the number and quality of its stone carvings and gargoyles. The arches in the nave are supported by a veritable menagerie of animals and an upside-down 'falling man'. Near the north door, a dragon-like creature emerges from a man's mouth while over the pulpit a monstrous face fixes the congregation with its single eye. Around the base of the font are eight heads all with their tongues poking out – a popular image of the time which some scholars believe is a sanitized version of earlier phallic carvings. Similarly, the girning faces are a bowdlerized rendering of the female sexual organs. Outside, there's a gruesome gathering of gargoyles leering and grimacing at all who approach.

In the centre of the village, the old stocks and whipping post have survived, along with the stump of a fourteenth-century cross.

OTHER PLACES
OF INTEREST

Belvoir Castle
(p. 14) and Plungar
(p. 92) to the south-
west.

BRADGATE HOUSE

The Nine Days' Queen

23

Location: *There are
three entrances to
Bradgate Park. The
nearest to Bradgate
House is on the
B5327 in the centre
of Newtown
Linford*
MAP REFERENCE:
129: 535103

Poor Lady Jane Grey! Her first misfortune was to have as father the scheming and ambitious Duke of Suffolk who made her childhood a misery. Lady Jane confided to her tutor that in her father's presence she must do everything 'even so perfectly as God made the world – or else I am so sharply taunted, so cruelly threatened, yea presently sometimes with pinches, nippes, and other ways I will not name, that I think myself in hell'.

Worse was to follow. At the age of 16 she was forced against her will to marry the son of the Duke of Northumberland, Regent to Edward VI. With his own eye on power, Northumberland prevailed on the dying Edward to name Jane as heir to the throne. On hearing that she had been proclaimed Queen, she fell fainting to the ground. Public opinion recognized Mary Tudor as the rightful heir and within days both Jane's father and father-in-law had deserted her. Jane spent nine days as a reluctant Queen and a further seven months as a prisoner in the Tower of London – before a swift death on the executioner's block on 12 February 1554. Today, the lovely rose-red ruins of Bradgate House where Jane passed much of her brief, unhappy life look too benign and inviting ever to have been involved in such a murderous tale of sixteenth-century politics.

*OTHER PLACES
OF INTEREST*

*Swithland (p. 107)
to the north; Anstey
(p. 1) and Leicester
(p. 54) to the south-
east; Kirby Muxloe
(p. 52) to the south-
west.*

BRADGATE PARK

The Folly of Old John

Although 'Old John' is one of the most distinctive landmarks in the county, its origins remain obscure. It stands on the loftiest point in this extensive public park, at first glance an old tower flanked by a ruined arch. A second look suggests an ale tankard with the arch as its handle. This sly inference may have been what the 5th Earl of Stamford had in mind when he built the folly in 1784 in memory of a former member of his household. An alternative version states that when the Earl came of age, a huge bonfire was lit, 'in the middle of which was erected a large pole, surrounded by tar-barrels, faggots etc; the pole being burnt through at the bottom, fell on the old man and killed him'. If this is true, the memorial acquires a more sombre hue.

The largest park in the county, covering some 800 acres of wooded hills and craggy outcrops of rock, Bradgate was a gift to the people of Leicestershire from Charles Bennion of the British United Shoe Machinery Company. Within its boundaries are the remains of Bradgate House (*see previous page*) where the 'Nine Days' Queen', Lady Jane Grey, spent much of her short life.

OTHER PLACES OF INTEREST

Swithland (p. 107) to the north; Anstey (p. 1) and Leicester (p. 54) to the south-east; Kirby Muxloe (p. 52) to the south-west.

BRAUNSTON

A 'Sheela-na-Gig' by the Church

Location:
Braunston is on an
unclassified road
about 2 miles south-
west of Oakham
MAP REFERENCE:
141: 832067

It stands against the west wall of the church, a powerful and disturbing figure. It's clearly female but estimates of its age vary from the Iron Age to the fourteenth century. One popular explanation is that the carving is a pagan fertility symbol, an Earth Mother of unique style. But the consensus seems to be that the figure is a Sheela-na-Gig, the discreetly modified form of the pagan sculptures allowed by the early Church, usually in the form of gargoyles (*see also* Bottesford, p. 22). The explicit nature of the pagan fertility symbols was suppressed in favour of female forms 'who evoke their fecundity by using their hands to prominently display other parts of their anatomy' – usually their mouths.

This extraordinary carving was discovered early this century when repairs were being carried out on the church. The figure had been laid face down and used as a threshold in the porch.

OTHER PLACES
OF INTEREST

Oakham (p. 87) and
Burley on the Hill
(p. 29) to the north-
east; Uppingham
(p. 114) to the
south; Launde (p.
53) to the south-
east.

BREEDON ON THE HILL

The Angel of Blessing

Location: The
church is just to the
west of the A453
Nottingham–Ashby
de la Zouch road.
Turn off at the
village green and
follow the road up
the hill
MAP REFERENCE:
129: 406235

If you want a dramatic site for a church, look no further than St Mary's at Breedon on the Hill. In this low-lying country, it sits atop a sudden ridge that rises 180 ft from the plain, a position emphasized on one side by a deep lime-quarry that has gnawed away half the hill.

Inside the church you'll find some of the finest Saxon sculptures in England. If we knew the sculptors' names, they would be seriously famous. Twelve hundred years after they laid down their chisels, one is still moved by their subtle work – dancers, birds, complicated marginal decorations and, most touching of all, the figure of a single angel with flowers strewn at her feet. She stands almost one metre high and by modern standards she is plump – 'the face is heavy and succulently rounded', says Pevsner, 'and the arms and hands are fleshy'. But the spirit that emanates from this simple carving is strong, direct and irresistible.

Many of the figures are in the chancel and easily visible but the angel is placed in the bell-ringing tower – the keys are available from the churchwardens.

OTHER PLACES
OF INTEREST

Castle Donington
(p. 32) to the north;
Belton (p. 13) to the
south-east; Staunton
Harold (p. 102) to
the south-west.

BROOKSBY

A Man of Effeminate Beauty

Location: Brooksby
is located just off
the A607 Melton
Mowbray–Leicester
road, about 6 miles
west of Melton
MAP REFERENCE:
129: 671160

For almost five hundred years the Villiers family had a manor house at Brooksby. Their wealth came from large land-holdings across the county but their fortunes took a dizzying leap early in the reign of James I. Young George Villiers, 'a man possessed of effeminate beauty', was presented at Court and for King James it was a case of love at first sight. Within seven years, the country squire's son had hurtled up the slippery pole of Court preferment to become the 1st Duke of Buckingham.

The King's infatuation never faltered. He ends one letter to his protégé with the words 'God bless you, my sweet child and wife, and grant that ye may ever be a comfort to your dear dad and husband'. Even after the accession of Charles I, George maintained his powerful position but his deeply unpopular policies led to his assassination in 1628. His descendants continued to live at Brooksby until the line came to an end with the death of Sir William Villiers in 1711. It is to Sir William, the last of the Villiers, that the grand grey and white marble monument in St Michael's Church is dedicated.

Brooksby Hall is now an Agricultural College but the church next to it is open to the public.

OTHER PLACES
OF INTEREST

Gaddesby (p. 44) to
the south; Rearsby
(p. 93) to the south-
west; Thrussington
(p. 110) to the west.

BROUGHTON ASTLEY

George Fox's Debut Speech

Location: From the A426, 10 miles south of Leicester, take the B581 towards Stoney Stanton for about 3 miles. Quaker Cottage, 140: 523937, is about 1 mile north-west of Broughton Astley village

MAP REFERENCE: 140: 527927

It was at Broughton Astley in 1647, at a gathering of Baptists and other dissenters, that the 23-year-old George Fox made his first major public speech. The fiery orator was still formulating the principles of what would later become the Quaker philosophy but his fulminations against the Established Church and its 'steeple-houses' were received with acclaim. 'In that day the Lord's power began to spring,' he wrote, '– several were convinced in these parts and turned from darkness to light.'

One of those who saw the light that day was Edward Erbury whose house, now called Quaker Cottage, still stands in the hamlet of Sutton in the Elms. Edward was the leading figure in the village's Quaker community which remained steadfast despite constant harassment. On 22 June 1679 he

and fifteen others were holding a meeting in his cottage when an informer burst in with the local constable. Edward was fined £20, an enormous sum then and one which he did not possess. Bailiffs were sent to seize the contents of his cottage, a task they carried out with such enthusiasm that they even removed the bed from under his sick wife, depositing her on the floor.

OTHER PLACES OF INTEREST

Blaby (p. 20) to the north-east; Bitteswell (p. 19) and Lutterworth (p. 70) to the south; Elmesthorpe (p. 39) to the west.

BURLEY ON THE HILL

A Famous Village Smithy

Location: Burley
village is on the
B668, about 2.5
miles north-east of
Oakham
MAP REFERENCE:
130: 883107

It's a sad fact that Rutland's grandest house is not open to the public. Burley on the Hill House is visible for miles around, high on its ridge above Rutland Water. It was built using local Clipsham stone between 1674 and 1704 for Daniel Finch, 2nd Earl of Nottingham, and it was constructed on an heroic scale. The vast Doric colonnades on the north front are a precise copy of those at St Peter's in Rome and the house stands in the middle of a thousand acres of parkland surrounded by a wall 6 miles long.

The church at Burley is usually closed. That's also a shame since it contains a touching memorial to Lady Charlotte Finch, governess to the children of King George III. Carved in white marble by Sir Francis Chantrey, it shows the kneeling figure of a beautiful young woman. Since the sculptor could not have met her until she was in her sixties at least, some artistic licence was obviously invoked but contemporaries all spoke of Lady Charlotte as 'a lovely and virtuous lady'.

What you can see is the old smithy on the village green which, it is claimed, was the inspiration for the song 'Underneath the spreading chestnut tree'. During the 1930s, the smithy was used in the advertisements for Cherry Blossom Boot Polish.

OTHER PLACES
OF INTEREST

Exton (p. 41) and
Greetham (p. 46) to
the north-east;
Oakham (p. 87) and
Braunston (p. 25) to
the south-west;
Wymondham
(p. 118) to the
north-west.

BURROUGH ON THE HILL

Location: From the
A606, about 5 miles
south of Melton
Mowbray, turn right
on to an unclassified
road to Somerby,
then follow signs for
'Burrough Hill
Country Park'
MAP REFERENCE:
129: 759119

Leicestershire's Grand National

Windswept, bleak, and 700 ft high, Burrough Hill commands views over vast areas of north-western Leicestershire and the County Council has helpfully provided a toposcope identifying places in the panorama. The strategic value of these heights was recognized very early on for it was here, some time in the 3rd century BC, that the Coritani tribe built a massive fort. Many of its imposing ramparts, up to 20 ft high, still stand, presenting the most clearly defined and best preserved Iron Age fort in the Midlands. Abandoned in Roman times, the hill top later became a popular location for fairs, festivals and steeple-chasing. Edward VIII, as Prince of Wales, often rode in point-to-points here and it

was while staying at Burrough Court that he met Mrs Wallis Simpson for the first time. The horse-riding connection is further enhanced by the fact that the 1873 Grand National was held here although it is difficult to work out exactly where the course would have been.

OTHER PLACES
OF INTEREST

Burton Lazars (next
page) and Little
Dalby (p. 67) to the
north; Gaddesby
(p. 44) to the north-
west.

BURTON LAZARS

A Monumental Overspending

Location: Burton
Lazars is on the
A606 Melton–
Oakham road,
approximately 2
miles south of
Melton. The
churchyard is just to
the west of the main
road
MAP REFERENCE:
129: 765169

Burton Lazars derives its unusual name from the leper hospital dedicated to St Lazarus that stood here from 1135 to 1544, the largest and richest of all the lazar houses in England. Its wealth stemmed from a generous endowment in 1193 when Roger de Mowbray founded the charity as thanks for his safe return from the second Crusade.

Nothing now remains of the great hospital which stood about 350 yd west of St James' Church but the village is well worth visiting just to see the exuberant monument in the graveyard to William Squire who died in 1781. Originally gilded and painted, this 'gingerbread tomb' includes almost every device fashionable in funerary art at the time – a pyramid, urn, sarcophagus, eagles, serpents, a globe, angels, crosses and, of course, the obligatory skull and bones. William, a weaver, had amassed a fortune of about £600 and had intended this to be divided between paying for the memorial and a legacy to provide education for poor children. In the event, by the time the monument was completed there were no funds left for the children.

OTHER PLACES
OF INTEREST
Little Dalby
(p. 67) to the south-
west; Melton
Mowbray (p. 77) to
the north-west.

CASTLE DONINGTON

Location: On the
north-west edge of
the county, 3 miles
west of the M1
(Junction 24)
MAP REFERENCE:
129: 445273

A Recycled Pulpit

Castle Donington is best known nowadays as a motor-racing circuit but in the 1860s it was far more notorious in society circles as the home of the wastrel 4th Marquis of Hastings. At the age of 17 the Marquis had inherited a respected title (his great-grandfather had been Governor-General of India), and a colossal fortune (for the same reason). With a dedication worthy of a better cause, the Marquis set about destroying both in a spectacular career of dissipation and reckless gambling – his betting on the 1866 Derby alone left him £140,000 poorer. Even the usually fawning obituary in *The Times* had to admit that the Marquis 'was as prodigal of his honour as of his wealth'.

What a contrast with the life of the Revd John Dalby, vicar of Castle Donington at that time. Modest, temperate and frugal, he was the model of a late-Victorian vicar, serving his parish for forty-five years. But his admiring parishioners were taken aback when they learnt that the Dalby family's monument to their father was to be a pulpit spatch-cocked from slabs of memorial stones being removed from the church floor during restoration. 'These were fine alabaster slabs,' protested one of his sons, rejecting criticism that the family had been economizing on the truth. 'If we hadn't used them, they would have been lost for ever.'

OTHER PLACES
OF INTEREST

Belton (p. 13) to the
south-east; Breedon
on the Hill (p. 26)
to the south;
Staunton Harold
(p. 102) to the
south-west.

CHURCH LANGTON

Horticulture and Hallelujahs

Location: *From the A6, 5 miles north of Market Harbough, turn right on the B6047 to Church Langton (2.5 miles)* MAP REFERENCE: 141: 724934

The Revd William Hanbury, rector of St Peter's, Church Langton, from 1753 until 1778 had two consuming passions in life: music and horticulture. The author of *A Complete Body of Planting and Gardening*, William was accused of neglecting his flock in favour of tending the many thousands of plants in his nurseries. There was considerable local opposition when he commandeered the village green and covered it with thousands of saplings. William suffered natural reverses as well. The winter of 1763/4 was unusually wet – six thousand young peach trees perished. In the following spring caterpillars destroyed ten thousand apple trees.

Running short of money, William hit upon the idea of an annual music festival in the church in order to raise funds and also to advertise the shrubs, trees and plants on sale in his nurseries. It was at one of these concerts, in September 1759, that an audience of some two thousand people heard Handel's *Messiah* – its first performance outside London.

There is a small bust of William Hanbury in the church and a memorial window at the east end commemorates this engaging and energetic enthusiast.

OTHER PLACES OF INTEREST

Hallaton (p. 48) and Medbourne (p. 75) to the east; Market Harborough (p. 72) to the south; Foxton (p. 43) to the south-west.

CLAYBROOKE MAGNA

A Working Water Mill

Location:
Claybrooke Magna
is on the B577
between
Lutterworth and
Ermine Street (A5).
The mill is on
Frolesworth Lane,
an unclassified road,
about 1 mile north-
east of the village.
MAP REFERENCE:
140: 499891

The old mill on a tributary of the River Soar at Claybrooke Magna is Leicestershire's only working water mill. There has been a mill on this site since at least the thirteenth century but the present structure dates from the 1700s. The mill ceased production in 1953 but it was restored in 1988 and is now working again. The stone-ground flour it produces is once again on sale. The three-storey building houses an internal overshot wooden wheel and can be viewed by appointment with the proprietor, David Mountford, telephone (01455) 202443.

Curiously, Claybrooke Magna has no church, but Claybrooke Parva does. It was the scene of another curious ecclesiastical punishment (*see also* Ashby de la Zouch and Stoke Golding). In this instance, in the 1780s, the offenders were a man and a woman found guilty of fornication. The rector, the Revd Auley Macaulay – brother of the more famous Lord Macaulay – reported that 'they both did public penance by standing in the middle aisle during the time of Divine Service, invested with white sheets'. He went on to observe: 'If the discipline of the Church in this and other matters were strictly enforced, it might tend to give some check to that unbridled licentiousness of manners which has of late pervaded our villages.'

OTHER PLACES
OF INTEREST

Broughton Astley
(p. 28) to the north-
east; Bitteswell
(p. 19) and
Lutterworth (p. 70)
to the south-east.

CLIPSHAM

A Treasury of Topiary

Location: From the
A1 at Stretton,
about 7 miles north-
west of Stamford,
take the unclassified
road eastwards to
Clipsham and
Castle Bytham.
About 1 mile past
Clipsham, the lodge
appears on the left
with a parking area
just beyond
MAP REFERENCE:
130: 978165

Amos Alexander, head forester to the Clipsham Hall Estate in the 1870s, loved topiary. Around his home, the lodge to Clipsham Hall, he clipped the yew trees into chimerical shapes – a fantastic parade of animals, chess pieces, or abstract forms such as the portly domes crowned with crosses or anvils. The Squire of Clipsham admired them greatly and gave Amos a free hand with the 150 yew trees lining the approach to the Hall. The results were spectacular. Along the 700 yd avenue appeared a dream-like succession of figures, some commemorating local or national events, others recording family events.

Amos died early this century and the trees went untended until in 1955 the Forestry Commission assumed responsibility for the avenue and renewed the topiary tradition. Each of the trees is about 15–20 ft high, and each is shaped individually. An elephant looks across to a ballerina, a Spitfire takes off towards a battleship, Diddy-men cavort near a windmill. This extraordinary spectacle is open, free, to the public: a walk up and down its length provides one of the most unusual promenades in the country.

OTHER PLACES
OF INTEREST

Tickencote (p. 111)
to the south; Exton
(p. 41) to the south-
west; Greetham
(p. 46) to the west.

DISHLEY

Location: The church ruins are just off a lay-by to the east of the A6, 1 mile south of Hathern, 2 miles north-west of Loughborough

MAP REFERENCE:
129: 513213

'The Great Improver'

The thirteenth-century church at Dishley is now just a ruin, its graveyard overgrown, its walls crumbling. Hardly anyone ever visits it but in the opinion of some this should be a major place of pilgrimage for here is a memorial to Robert Bakewell (1725–95) 'perhaps the greatest man ever born on Leicestershire soil'. Known as 'The Great Improver', Bakewell's fame derives from his success in the scientific breeding of livestock. At Dishley Grange nearby, he developed the New Leicester sheep by carefully monitored inbreeding. They caused an agricultural sensation because their barrel shape, short legs, small head and bones produced far more meat and fat – an average of 80 lb per sheep compared to the previous norm of 28 lb.

Bakewell also bred the forerunner of the noble Shire horse. Many of his stallions, bulls and rams were leased out to stud, one ram named 'Two-Pounder' earning him 1,200 guineas in one year. Despite such incomings, Bakewell was bankrupted in 1776, a result, it was said, of the generous hospitality he lavished on the unceasing stream of visitors (Russian princes, French and German dukes amongst them) who came to study his methods.

Just behind the church ruins stands a large square dovecote with a pyramid roof and white painted lantern built during the last years of Robert Bakewell's life.

OTHER PLACES OF INTEREST

Loughborough (p. 68) to the south-west; Belton (p. 13) to the west.

DONINGTON LE HEATH

'Uneasy Lies the Bed . . . '

Location: Just south
of Coalville off the
B585
MAP REFERENCE:
129: 421127

The oldest house in the county, the Manor House at Donington le Heath, was built around 1280. Now a museum, one of its most prized exhibits is 'King Richard's Bed', the bed in which Richard III is said to have slept the night before the Battle of Bosworth. The huge wooden bed had been brought from Nottingham Castle and installed in the upper front room of the Blue Boar Inn in Leicester. The next day came the news of Richard's death and in the turmoil of a new reign nobody bothered to claim the bed. It passed down from landlord to landlord until, in 1613 when it was being moved, a gold coin fell from it. The landlady examined the bed more closely and discovered a secret drawer containing the then-colossal sum of £300 in gold.

Although the landlord, Thomas Clarke, and his wife told no one of their windfall, there was much talk of the Clarkes' sudden prosperity. But it wasn't until twenty years later that two men, in collusion with a maid, Alice, attacked Mrs Clarke, strangled her and made off with the remains of the hoard. The malefactors were quickly caught. One of the men, surprisingly, escaped punishment, but the other was hanged and Alice was burnt alive at the stake.

Opening times: Easter – September: 2.00 p.m. – 6.00 p.m. (Wednesday–Sunday, and Bank Holiday Mondays & Tuesdays).

OTHER PLACES
OF INTEREST

Appleby Magna (p.
2) and Appleby
Parva (p. 3) to the
south-west; Ashby
de la Zouch (p. 5) to
the north-west.

DRAYTON

The Smallest Church in the County

The church of St James at Drayton in the Welland Valley enjoys the distinction of being the smallest village church in Leicestershire. It's also probably the only church in the county to have been used as a bakehouse, a function it served for more than a hundred years. The Watson family of nearby Rockingham Castle paid for its restoration as a church and it was reconsecrated in 1879. It stands on the village green, a tiny single-cell building little more than 20 ft long and 12 ft wide, serving a population of less than two hundred. This miniature church was originally built as a 'chapel of ease' – a place of worship for those parishioners who lived too far from their parish church, in this case Bringhurst, just over a mile away.

OTHER PLACES OF INTEREST

Rockingham Castle (Northants) to the south-east; Hallaton (p. 48) and Medbourne (p. 75) to the north-west; Foxton (p. 43) to the south-west.

ELMESTHORPE

An 'Arts and Crafts' Village Inn

Location: From the A47, 4 miles north-east of Hinckley, turn right on the B581 for 1.5 miles. The inn is on the right, just after the railway bridge
MAP REFERENCE:
140: 470958

One of the leading lights in the late Victorian 'Arts and Crafts' movement pioneered by William Morris and John Ruskin was the architect C.F.A. Voysey (1857–1941). He was much in demand as a designer of country houses, many of which bore his distinctive stamp – steep, hipped roofs, huge tapering chimney stacks and the absence of the then-popular neo-Gothic decoration.

Voysey arrived in Elmesthorpe in 1895, summoned by the Earl of Lovelace who was then improving his estate. The Earl had commissioned Voysey to build six homes for artisans – 'Wortley Cottages' – and an inn, the Wentworth Arms near the railway station. The inn incorporates many of Voysey's favourite features: overhanging eaves, long, low dormer windows, an arcaded chimney breast and, inside, inglenook fireplaces, low ceilings and tiled hearths. Voysey declared that in his designs he 'strove to produce an effect of repose and simplicity', an effect he certainly achieved in his buildings at Elmesthorpe.

OTHER PLACES
OF INTEREST

Broughton Astley
(p. 28) to the south-east; Hinckley
(p. 50) to the south-west.

EMPINGHAM

A Dovecote on a Battlefield

Location:
Empingham lies just
off the A606, about
half-way between
Oakham and
Stamford. From the
High Street, take the
minor road running
north, just east of
the church. The
dovecote is in a field
about 100 yd up on
the right
MAP REFERENCE:
141: 955089

In a field just outside the village of Empingham stands a magnificent stone dovecote containing seven hundred nests. It could serve as a symbolic memorial to the ten thousand men who were killed nearby in one of the bloodiest slaughters of the Wars of the Roses. The Battle of Losecoat Field was fought on 12 March 1470 and took its name from the fact that the defeated Lancastrians shed their uniforms to avoid recognition, capture and certain death.

Empingham has always been one of Rutland's most important villages with one of its largest churches. Even at the time of the Domesday Book it had a population of five hundred and at least twelve mills. The village later became part of the Normanton Park estate and its population was considerably increased in 1764 when Sir Gilbert Heathcote removed the people of Normanton *en masse* to Empingham in order to improve the view from his Hall.

OTHER PLACES
OF INTEREST

Tickencote (p. 111)
to the north-east;
Normanton
(p. 85) to the south-
west; Exton (p. 41)
to the north-west.

EXTON

'The Admiration of his Contemporaries'

Location: From the
A1 at Stretton, go
west on the B668.
About 1 mile past
Greetham turn left
on an unclassified
road to Exton. The
church is signposted
in the village
MAP REFERENCE:
130: 920112

Charmingly set in parkland, the church of St Peter and St Paul at Exton is remarkable for its wealth of fine monuments. Rivalling those at Bottesford, this sumptuous series commemorates members of the Noel and Harington families interred here from the early sixteenth to the late eighteenth century. This imposing collection is dominated by the colossal memorial to Baptist Noel, 3rd Viscount Campden, Lord Lieutenant of Rutland, who died in 1683. Sculpted in black and white marble by Grinling Gibbons, it stands 22 ft high and 14 ft wide, almost filling one wall of the north transept. Two larger than life statues of the Viscount and his fourth wife stand above wreathed panels in which are represented his other three wives and his nineteen children. A lengthy inscription records the family's losses in the Royalist cause during the Civil War – the 'spoil and havock of several of his houses' – and Viscount Campden's many qualities which 'have justly rendered him the admiration of his contemporaries and the imitation of posterity'.

OTHER PLACES
OF INTEREST

Stretton (p. 105) to
the north-east;
Tickencote (p. 111)
to the south-east;
Oakham (p. 87) to
the south-west.

FENNY DRAYTON

The Birthplace of George Fox

Location: From the A5, about 7 miles north-west of Hinckley, turn right on the A444 to Fenny Drayton (about 1 mile)
MAP REFERENCE: 140: 351971

George Fox's teenage years were a time of acute civil and religious tensions and he did nothing to help calm them when, in 1643 at the age of 19, he began preaching vehemently against a 'Church corrupted' and a State that legitimized warfare and capital punishment. Such views were not uncommon at the time but George presented them with a mystical, sometimes impenetrable, rhetoric and with a curious admixture of other notions. Removing one's hat to anyone, for example, was anathema; bowing was the 'effect of Satanical influence'; to speak of the month of March was to worship Mars, the God of War; to refer to Monday was paying idolatrous homage to the moon. George's extraordinary compôte of social ideas well ahead of their time and half-baked prejudices was expressed with such passion that his whole body quaked – hence the soubriquet attached ever since to the Society of Friends.

George Fox was born at Fenny Drayton in 1624 and baptized in the font that stands on a wooden plinth against the west wall of the Church of St Michael and All Angels. The family house has disappeared but there is a memorial stone to him in the grounds of Monument House at the junction of George Fox Lane and Old Forge Yard.

OTHER PLACES OF INTEREST

Bilstone (p. 18) to the north; Sutton Cheney (p. 106) to the north-east; Hinckley (p. 50) to the south-east.

FOXTON

A Staircase on the Canal

43

Location: From the A6, 2 miles north of Market Harborough, turn left on an unclassified road for about 3 miles. The locks are widely signposted
MAP REFERENCE:
141: 691894

During the great age of canal-building in the early nineteenth century, the Grand Junction Canal from the Thames in London to the industrial Midlands was progressing smoothly across the lowlands of central England until it came to the 75 ft high limestone ridge near Foxton. This was the kind of natural obstacle that had brought many canal projects to a dead end, but the directors of the company called upon one of the most gifted engineers of the time – Thomas Telford – to resolve the problem. He came up with an inspired solution – a staircase of locks. There are ten of them in all, in two blocks of five with a passing pool between them (and a pub, *Bridge 61*, at the bottom). Because the flight was so expensive to build, the channel was restricted to a breadth of 7 ft which became the standard width of passage for a 'narrow boat'. Nowadays, no canal boat owners can be considered fully fledged until they have navigated their way up or down this extraordinary ladder of water.

OTHER PLACES OF INTEREST

Church Langton (p. 33) to the north; Hallaton (p. 48) and Medbourne (p. 75) to the north-east; Market Harborough (p. 72) to the south-east.

GADDESBY

A Mighty Hero of Waterloo

Location: Gaddesby
lies just to the north
of the B674
Rearsby–Twyford
road

MAP REFERENCE:
129: 689131

It's the kind of white marble, life-sized statue that should really be placed somewhere surrounded by about 4 acres of open ground, not bursting the walls of St Luke's Church in Gaddesby. Colonel Edward Hawkins Cheney CB, of the Scots Greys, was one of the heroes of the Battle of Waterloo in 1815 – during the conflict, four horses died beneath him and a fifth was wounded. The colonel miraculously survived that carnage and, on his return to England, commissioned a fashionable sculptor of the time, Joseph Gott, to reproduce in fine marble the essence of his martial accomplishments. The statue was not originally intended for the church but for the colonel's residence, Gaddesby Hall, where for several years it was displayed in a conservatory. Then, around 1917, the monumental sculpture was put on rollers and dragged by hand from the Hall to the church.

OTHER PLACES
OF INTEREST

Brooksby (p. 27) to
the north; Little
Dalby (p. 67) to the
north-east; Beeby
(p. 11) to the south;
Rearsby (p. 93) and
Thrussington
(p. 110) to the
north-west.

GLENFIELD

The Longest Tunnel in England

July 17th 1832 was a great day for Glenfield, at that time a quiet village some 3 miles north of Leicester. For it was here that the first, and for many a year the longest, railway tunnel in England – 1 mile 36 yd long – was about to be formally opened. It had been designed by no less a personage than George Stephenson's son, Robert. A celebratory train, headed by a covered carriage for the directors, followed by ten open coal wagons for the public and a brass band 'that accompanied our passage

with the most soothing melodies', chuffed its way through the horse-shoe shaped entrance to this latest marvel of English engineering.

Today, the tunnel opening is blocked. The last fare-paying passenger travelled through it on 24 September 1928, the last goods train on 6 December 1965. Four years after that, Leicester City Council paid British rail £5 to acquire and preserve this unique relic of railway history. It's now swamped by a modern housing estate but if you can find the entrance it's still an imposing sight.

OTHER PLACES
OF INTEREST

Anstey (p. 1) and
Bradgate Park
(p. 24) to the north;
Leicester (p. 54) to
the south-east;
Kirby Muxloe
(p. 52) to the south-
west.

GREETHAM

Early Evidence of Recycling

Location: From the
A1 at Stretton, go
west on the B668
for about 2 miles.
The house is in
Great Lane

MAP REFERENCE:
130: 920140

The village people of Greetham seem to have grasped the principles of recycling long before the rest of us. In the church, Saxon carvings and Norman mouldings from earlier churches on the site have been incorporated into the walls. And in Great Lane, the stonemason's house is adorned with an apparently random collection of masonry off-cuts.

At one time the village had no fewer than four public pumps. A fountain still survives, bearing this admonitory poem:

All ye who hither come to drink
Rest not your thoughts below
Remember Jacob's Well and think
Whence living waters flow.

OTHER PLACES
OF INTEREST

Stretton (p. 105)
and Clipsham
(p. 35) to the north-
east; Exton (p. 41)
to the south; Burley
on the Hill (p. 29)
and Oakham (p. 87)
to the south-west.

GRIMSTON

Bidding by Candle

Location: From the
junction of the
A6006 and the
B676 near Six Hills,
take the old Salt
Road eastwards
towards Ab
Kettleby. After
about 1.5 mile, turn
right to Grimston
MAP REFERENCE:
129: 685219

Perhaps because of its unappealing name, Grimston tends to be overlooked by guide books. Even that indefatigable chronicler Arthur Mee omits it from his 'King's England' book. Grimston is, in fact, one of the county's most attractive villages. At its centre is a lovely green where a set of ancient stocks stands beneath a chestnut tree. Overlooking the green are two venerable hostelries and the Church of St John the Evangelist. Here the curious custom of 'bidding by candle' continued until the early years of this century. A small stump of candle was lit and buyers would then make their bids for the item being auctioned. Whoever made the last bid before the candle went out acquired the lot at that price.

OTHER PLACES
OF INTEREST

Melton Mowbray
(p. 77) to the south-
east; Brooksby
(p. 27) and
Thrussington
(p. 110) to the
south; Barrow upon
Soar (p. 8) and
Loughborough
(p. 68) to the south-
west.

HALLATON

Location: Hallaton
is about 6 miles
south-west of
Uppingham, via the
B664 and an
unclassified road
MAP REFERENCE:
141: 786966

A Pagan Survival

Every Easter Monday, the old Buttercross in the lovely little village of Hallaton is the setting for the crowning ceremony of the Hare-Pie Scrambling and Bottle-Kicking contest. The captain of the winning team is lifted to the top of the conical monument and there he broaches a bottle of ale. The contest is a free-for-all struggle between the neighbouring villages of Hallaton and Medbourne to get two out of three bottles of ale across the village boundary by whatever means possible. (The 'bottles' are actually small oak casks.) As many as four hundred players may be milling around in the scrum and the battle has been known to continue for eight or nine hours.

The ceremony begins with a procession through the village to Hare-Pie Bank where the pieces of a huge hare pie are thrown to the crowd. The bottle-kicking can then begin. According to Charles Bilson in his *Vestiges of Paganism in Leicestershire* (1911), the custom is a 'maimed and distorted' relic of a 'dim and distant age when the inhabitants of this island actually worshipped the hare as a divine animal, and in the springtime held a religious procession and annual sacrifice of the god'. That may explain the hare pie, but the origins of the bottle-kicking remain mysterious.

OTHER PLACES
OF INTEREST

Launde (p. 53) to
the north; Oakham
(p. 87) to the north-
east; Uppingham
(p. 114) to the east;
Drayton (p. 38) and
Medbourne (p. 75)
to the south;
Church Langton
(p. 33) to the south-
west.

HEMINGTON

A Ruinous Dwelling

Location: From Exit 24 of the M1, take the A6 towards Derby, then almost immediately turn left on an unclassified road through Lockington to Hemington. At the T-junction turn left towards Castle Donington then left again
MAP REFERENCE: 129: 457278

As long ago as 1590, Henry Wyrley reported that in Hemington church 'the glass was all ruined and the church not in use'. It's not clear why it was allowed to reach this ruinous state but during the latter part of the nineteenth century the remains provided a convenient dwelling for an old woman who installed herself in the chancel. Officious authorities insisted that she be removed to a workhouse.

The shell of the church's 50 ft high tower stood for some seven hundred years and then suddenly collapsed after heavy spring rains in 1986. Overgrown with ivy, the remains now present a supremely picturesque image of ruin and decay.

Just outside the village are the remains of Civil War trenches which were dug in preparation for an attack on Hemington Hall, the residence of Sir John Harpur-Crewe whose family later achieved a certain fame as the owners of Calke Abbey. Part of Hemington village still belongs to the Harpur-Crewe estate.

OTHER PLACES OF INTEREST

Castle Donington (p. 32) to the south; Breedon-on-the-Hill (p. 26) to the south-west

Location: The
churchyard is in the
centre of Hinckley,
just south of the
A47
MAP REFERENCE:
140: 432941

HINCKLEY

A Tombstone that Bled

During the mid-1700s, gossip across the county told of a tombstone in Hinckley churchyard that dripped blood. It was a memorial to a young man killed in a public house by a recruiting sergeant he had offended by some 'trifling joke'. The inscription reads:

HERE LIETH THE BODY OF RICHARD SMITH WHO DEPARTED THIS LIFE
THE 12TH DAY OF AUGUST 1727 IN THE 20TH YEAR OF HIS AGE.

> A fatal halberd this body slew
> The murdering hand God's vengeance will pursue
> From shades terrene though justice took her flight
> Shall not the judge of all the world do right?
> Each age and sex his innocence bemoans
> And with sad sighs lament his dying groans.

The violence of the young man's death lent credence to the notion of a bleeding tombstone but sadly a local historian, A.J. Pickering, has come up with a more mundane explanation. 'Richard Smith's tombstone,' he explains, 'used to abut the east end of the church and it was frequently noticed to be spattered with red spots. The superstitious of course took this for blood but I believe it came from the ironstone in the church wall above.' The stone has now been moved away from the wall, and the 'bleeding' has been staunched.

OTHER PLACES
OF INTEREST

Sutton Cheney
(p. 106) and Stoke
Golding (p. 104) to
the north;
Elmesthorpe (p. 39)
to the north-east;
Broughton Astley
(p. 28) to the east;
Bitteswell (p. 19)
and Lutterworth
(p. 70) to the south-
east.

KETTON

A Master Mason's Memorial

Location: Ketton is on the A6121 Stamford–Uppingham road, about 5 miles west of Stamford. The Hibbins' house is by the main crossroads in the village; the church just down the hill from there
MAP REFERENCE:
141: 982043

The buildings of Ketton are remarkably handsome. This is not altogether a surprise since in the hills just outside the village is quarried the famous butter-coloured stone which has been used in cathedrals (Ely, Peterborough), stately homes (Belton House, Burley on the Hill), Cambridge colleges (Clare Hall, Trinity College Library) and public buildings such as the Houses of Parliament. The durable stone was also used for gravestones and St Mary's churchyard displays some fine examples of the stonemason's work. Several generations of the Hibbins family worked as masons in the area so it's appropriate that William Hibbins' monument is particularly striking. It stands in a rank of gravestones by the lych-gate and although rather weatherbeaten still clearly shows the tools of the mason's trade – dividers, a square, hammer, pick and chisel. Just up the road from the church, William's descendants built a house on Stocks Hill rich in architectural detail and with their surname prominently displayed in stone relief above the front door.

In the 1950s, incidentally, Ketton could boast that all of the three factory chimneys in Rutland were located there, as well as the only set of traffic lights in the county.

OTHER PLACES OF INTEREST
Empingham (p. 40) and Tickencote (p. 111) to the north; Uppingham (p. 114) to the south-west; Wing (p. 117) to the west; Normanton (p. 85) to the north-west.

KIRBY MUXLOE

An Uncompleted Castle

Location: 5 miles
east of Leicester on
the A47, turn right
on the B5380, then
follow signs for the
castle.

MAP REFERENCE:
140: 524046

In the Court of King Edward IV, William, Lord Hastings was known as a 'faithful servant, a man of honour, influence and prudence'. Under the King's patronage, he accumulated offices that were both powerful and profitable – Chamberlain of the Royal Household, Master of the Mint, Chamberlain of the North – and in 1480 was granted permission to build a fortified mansion at Kirby Muxloe. A mere three years later the 41-year-old King died suddenly, 'worn out by his debaucheries', and Richard III seized power. Within weeks Hastings had been summarily executed. Shakespeare depicts Richard confronting Hastings with the words: 'Thou art a traitor. Off with his head. Now by St Paul I swear will not dine until I see the same.'

Work on the unfinished castle ground to a halt and was never resumed. Nowadays the only substantial remains are those of the gatehouse and the three-storey western tower. Built in glowing red Leicestershire brick and surrounded by a moat, they're an evocative testimony to the perilous nature of fifteenth-century English politics.

For current opening times call English Heritage (0116) 938 6886.

OTHER PLACES
OF INTEREST

Glenfield (p. 45)
and Anstey (p. 1) to
the north-east;
Leicester (p. 54) to
the east; Sutton
Cheney (p. 106) to
the south-west.

LAUNDE ABBEY

An 'Item to Remember'

Location: 8 miles
west of Uppingham
on the A47, turn
right on an
unclassified road to
Loddington and
then Launde
MAP REFERENCE:
141: 797044

'Item to remember,' wrote Thomas Cromwell in his diary for 1536, 'Launde for myself.' Thomas, Henry VIII's avaricious Chancellor, had just visited the lovely old Launde Priory, founded in 1125. It was a fine building, set in a beautiful position on a grassy plain (a launde, or lawn) and surrounded by woods – Thomas 'much coveted it'. The Prior detected the Chancellor's interest and recorded that the King's agent was 'a man of prying eyes and gripple (grasping) hands'. Discreetly, the Prior began squirrelling away the Priory's treasures into the care of trusted friends. At the Dissolution of the Monasteries, Cromwell did indeed take

Launde for himself, but within months he had fallen from favour and was beheaded in 1540.

Since then, the building has been extensively altered and restored, and is now an Anglican house of retreat, still evoking a sense of deep and untroubled peace. Launde's chapel, which can be visited on request, contains a fine monument to Gregory Cromwell (son of Thomas) which Pevsner asserts is 'one of the purest monuments of the early Renaissance in England'.

OTHER PLACES
OF INTEREST

Oakham (p. 87) to
the north-east;
Hallaton (p. 48) and
Medbourne (p. 75)
to the south-east;
Billesdon (p. 16) to
the west.

LEICESTER

Thomas Cook's Four-Part Frieze

A golden rule when exploring an unfamiliar city is to keep your eyes raised above the ground floor. At that level, you will only see the usual succession of humdrum shop-fronts, many of them replicated across the country. But very often they are just facades stuck onto genuinely interesting buildings – as with the Singer Building and the Turkey Café in Leicester (*see* pp. 62, 64). Shop-window gazers will also miss the curious four-part frieze on the former travel offices of Thomas Cook in Gallowtree Gate, just across from the Clock Tower.

The extreme left plaque represents Cook's (and the world's) first excursion train, which ran from Leicester to Loughborough on 5 July 1841. 570 'Friends of Temperance' crowded into open wagons, having paid one shilling each for the 13 mile return journey to attend a four-hour temperance rally. The second plaque shows an excursion train on its way to the Great Exhibition of 1851. More than 165,000 passengers used the company's trains and transformed 'Cook's Tours' into a national institution. The third plaque is dated 1884, the year in which Thomas Cook was asked by the Army to arrange transport along the River Nile for troops attempting to rescue General Gordon in Khartoum. The final plaque commemorates the travel firm's fiftieth anniversary in 1891.

LEICESTER

Entertainment at the Gaol

Visitors to Leicester frequently mistake the Welford Road prison with its crenellated towers and stone portcullis for Leicester Castle. Some have even enquired about its opening times. The imposing building was completed in 1828 at a time when executions were still conducted in public, providing a change of pace from the customary entertainments of bear-baiting, cock-fighting and watching terriers let loose in a rat-pit. The scaffold was erected in front of the main entrance and patients in the Royal Infirmary opposite gathered at their windows to enjoy a particularly fine view of the event.

The last person to be hanged here was William Brown in 1856. In a dispute at Thorpe Arnold tollgate, 'Peppermint' Billy had shot the gatekeeper and cut the throat of his 8-year-old grandson. The double murder had excited great interest and the crowd was numbered at more than 25,000 people. Brown's father was amongst them and after watching the execution he exclaimed, 'Well done, Billy, tha died a brick!'

LEICESTER

The Beaumanor Chair

One of the most extraordinary chairs ever built, the Beaumanor Chair has the appearance of an exploded crown and certainly doesn't look as if it were designed for comfort. And indeed it wasn't. It was presented to the Herricks of Beaumanor Hall (*see* p. 10) by another local family, the Farnhams, as a year's rent for lands they held known as Rushy Fields. Dated 1690, the huge semi-throne was cut from the solid trunk of a single oak, 37 ft in circumference, and decorated with the Herrick family motto '*Virtus omnia nobilitate*' and a carved garland of roses surrounding a spear and an arrow head.

The unique chair was only one of the unorthodox forms of rent received by the Herricks. A tenant at Barrow upon Soar paid his dues with a pound of pepper, not a trifling expense in those days; another from Frisby delivered four flights of arrows each year in lieu of ancient feudal services.

The Beaumanor Chair is now housed in the Newarke Houses Museum.

LEICESTER

'The Heaviest Man That Ever Lived'

When Daniel Lambert died on 21 June 1809 at the Wagon and Horses Inn at Stamford there was a real problem. The deceased weighed 52 stones 11 pounds – at that time 'the heaviest man that ever lived'. A measuring tape wrapped around his waist only came to a stop when it had recorded 9 feet 4 inches. Each thigh was more than a yard in circumference. Newspaper reports of the time describe how a wall of the hotel had to be knocked down for the body to be removed (but they don't explain how Daniel managed to enter in the first place).

Daniel was born in Leicester in 1770. His parents were of normal size and so was he until, at the age of 20, he developed a medical condition that turned him into a freak. It wasn't drink: Daniel was a teetotaller. It wasn't over-eating: he was well known for his abstemious habits. Trapped inside his bloated body he could no longer continue his job as gaoler at Leicester prison, so this intelligent, cultivated man submitted to the indignity of being exhibited to visitors on payment of one shilling each. In the Newarke Houses Museum you can see his vast waistcoats and voluminous trousers – at the time they excited a prurient interest, now they only engender a sympathetic pity.

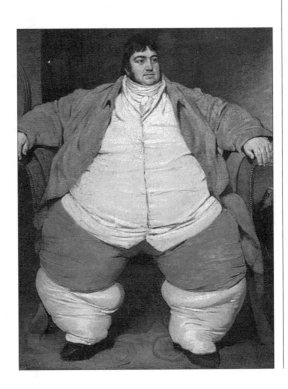

LEICESTER

A Celebrated Needlewoman

In the course of her long life – she died at the age of 90 – Mary Linwood became one of Leicester's most famous citizens. Her fame stemmed from her remarkable skills as a needlewoman, embroidering copies of well known paintings. Visitors to the permanent exhibition of her work in London declared that it was difficult to tell painting and embroidery apart. British and foreign royalty were much taken with her creations and in 1803 she was invited to dine with Napoleon in Paris. Following the meal, he conferred on her the Freedom of the City.

Mary lived and worked in Belgrave Gate where she also ran a private boarding school for girls. She was a familiar sight in the city as she was carried about in her sedan chair, one of the last in the country to remain in use. She never married and the lack of children to perpetuate her memory may have been the reason why Mary erected her own monument in St Margaret's Church long before her death in 1845. The simple epitaph added to the memorial to her parents reads 'Mary, their daughter, died in the nineteenth century'.

For other examples of pre-emptive memorials *see* Blaby (p. 20) and Swithland (p. 107).

TO THE MEMORY OF
MATTHEW LINWOOD,
WHO DEPARTED THIS LIFE
THE 28TH OF FEBRUARY, 1783;
AGED 56 YEARS.

ALSO
HANNAH, WIFE OF
MATTHEW LINWOOD,
WHO DIED
THE 28TH OF DECEMBER, 1804,
IN HER 80TH YEAR.

MARY, THEIR DAUGHTER,
DIED IN THE NINETEENTH CENTURY.

LEICESTER

The 'Pork Pie Chapel'

Joseph Hansom is probably best known for his 'Patent Safety (Hansom) Cab' designed in 1834. With its two huge 8 ft diameter wheels, the Hansom cab was a familiar sight on city streets until well into the twentieth century. (Cheated by the company formed to promote it, Hansom only received £300 for his comfortable invention.)

Hansom was also a highly regarded architect, with Birmingham Town Hall and Plymouth's Roman Catholic Cathedral amongst his many commissions. So in 1854 when the Baptist community in Leicester resolved to build a chapel in Belvoir Street they spared no expense in engaging one of the most prominent architects of the time. Working on a confined site, Hansom came up with an ingenious design that provided the semi-circular auditorium his patrons required. The town cynics, accustomed to seeing a more rectangular style dignifying Baptist places of worship, dubbed his creation the 'Pork Pie Chapel', an uncomplimentary epithet that only lost currency when the chapel closed in 1939. It later became an Adult Education Centre, the function it still serves.

LEICESTER

A Unique Promenade

One of the most elegant features of Georgian Leicester, New Walk, was laid out in 1785 as a pedestrian route from the city centre to the racecourse at what is now Victoria Park. Almost a mile long, it follows the route of the old Roman Road from Colchester to Chester, the *Via Devana*. Originally, the walk passed through open ground, but later houses were added piecemeal, although builders were not allowed to buy a second plot until they had sold the house(s) on the first. A public subscription raised £250 for trees and shrubs and nowadays the walk, unique in England, is a leafy avenue lined by an interesting medley of buildings (although some of the most recent developments are incongruous, to say the least).

To begin with, the promenade was known as Queen's Walk in honour of George III's wife, Charlotte. Later it was renamed Ladies Walk and, finally, New Walk. According to one Victorian resident, New Walk was 'the only solely respectable street in Leicester'. Midway along it stands the dignified City Museum with its huge Tuscan columns. This was built as a Nonconformist school in 1836 by J.A. Hansom (the inventor of the Hansom coach) who also built the 'Pork Pie' chapel in Belvoir Street (*see* p. 59).

LEICESTER

The Richest Man in Leicester

Leicester's Clock Tower is undeniably the focal point of the city but opinions differ as to its artistic merits: 'gaudy and grotesque' or 'wonderfully over-decorated' according to taste. Erected in 1868 to the design of a local architect, Joseph Goddard, each side features the statue of a celebrity or benefactor of the city. One of them is William Wyggeston, an immensely wealthy wool merchant who had the unusual distinction of being Mayor of Leicester twice (in 1499 and 1509), and Mayor of Calais, which was then an English possession, no fewer than four times.

William was by far the richest man in Leicester. The tax rolls for 1524 reveal that his assessment amounted to 22 per cent of the total raised in the city. William's bill was six times that of the next largest contributor, who happened to be his cousin. After his death in 1536, William's family devoted a substantial part of his fortune to founding a Free Grammar School. That building, erected in 1573, still stands in Highcross Street.

LEICESTER

An Exuberant Shop Front

At the turn of the century, one of the most sought-after consumer durables was a home sewing-machine. The most efficient model was undoubtedly the one invented in 1852 by the American Isaac Merritt Singer and for almost a hundred years his descendants enjoyed a virtual monopoly of the market. They spent their millions of profits with aplomb, whether in the casino at Monte Carlo or in erecting grandiose show-rooms for their products such as the one in High Street, Leicester.

They chose a local architect, Arthur Wakerley, who had already displayed talent with his Turkey Café in Granby Street (*see* p. 64). His Singer Building (1904) was equally exuberant. The ground floor has now been taken over by a random assortment of small businesses, but above them you can still see the proud Union Jack medallions with swags bearing the names of British possessions around the world – an Imperial celebration of the coronation of Edward VII.

Later, in the 1920s, Arthur became known nationally for designing a council house that could be built for £299. Complete with two bedrooms, internal coal bunker and a copper for wash-days, a bath tucked beside the kitchen, and a dustbin and rainwater butt fixed outside, it became a model for new municipal housing from Welwyn Garden City to Belfast.

LEICESTER

The 'Top Hat Terrace'

The first detective to be appointed when the Leicester Police Force was formed in 1836 was Francis Smith. He was notably successful in infiltrating the city gangs – like Sherlock Holmes he was a master of disguise. On his retirement in 1864, 'Tanky' Smith as he was known, set up as Leicester's first private detective and almost immediately made a reputation for himself by solving a Missing Person mystery. The missing person was no less than the High Sheriff of the County, James Beaumont Winstanley, who had gone missing on a European tour. Within days, Tanky had found his client – in Koblenz, unfortunately dead at the time and floating in the River Moselle.

Tanky invested his substantial fee for closing that particular file in building Victoria Terrace in London Road, a few hundred yards south of the railway station. His architect, who was also his son, paid tribute to his father's mastery of disguise by incorporating in the design sixteen stone heads, fifteen of them portraying one of Tanky's many disguises. The sixteenth shows Tanky wearing a top hat – a regulation item of a policeman's uniform until 1872 – so giving the row of houses its unofficial, later official, name of 'Top Hat Terrace'.

LEICESTER

The 'Turkey Café'

Amongst other achievements, Arthur Wakerley (1862–1931) was Leicester's youngest-ever Mayor. There's a photograph of him at the age of 35 looking insufferably self-satisfied in his municipal robes. The young architect already had quite a lot to be satisfied about. Since 1886 he had been successfully developing 5 acres of abandoned brick pits at North Evington on the edge of the city into his vision of a model community. Homes and shops, of course, but also factories, a market place and hall, a bank, dairy, 'coffee palace', and even a Salvation Army citadel. (But no pub. Arthur, like that other Leicester luminary Thomas Cook, was a teetotaller.)

One of Arthur Wakerley's most engaging buildings was the Turkey Café in Granby Street. Completed in 1901, it's an architectural *jeu d'esprit* with turkey motifs emblazoned in a colourful façade of Carrara-ware. For many years, the Turkey Café was *the* place in Leicester to take tea and coffee and it achieved an additional notoriety in 1966 when the owner, Luigi Brucciani, decided to reserve one of the rooms for Ladies Only. A female monitor was placed at the entrance with the sole purpose of forbidding entry to males. Her rôle was outlawed eight years later with the passing of the Sex Discrimination Act. The Turkey Café survived until 1982 when the premises were taken over by the opticians Rayners, who public-spiritedly spent £30,000 in restoring one of the city's most unusual buildings.

LEICESTER

A Powerful Guild

Location: On
Guildhall Lane,
next to St Martin's
Cathedral.

Leicester's black-and-white timbered Guildhall, nestling close to the Cathedral, is recognized as one of the most important surviving timber halls of the fourteenth century. It was built around 1350 by the Corpus Christi Guild, a group of the town's leading citizens attached to St Martin's Church (now the Cathedral). The Guild became such a significant power in the town that its two Masters took precedence over the Mayor. Since the Corporation had no hall of its own, it used the Guildhall for its council meetings. When the Corpus Christi Guild was dissolved at the Reformation, the Guildhall became the seat of the Town Council and served this function until a new Town Hall was built in 1876. The oldest part, the east end of the Great Hall, is marvellously atmospheric with its cruck beams, and there's some sumptuous carving and panelling in the Mayor's Parlour. The police cells on the ground floor, dating back to 1840, contain a fascinating collection of such penal hardware as gibbet-irons, thumbscrews and a scold's bridle.

For opening times telephone (0116) 265 0555.

LITTLE CASTERTON

Location: From the
A6121 Stamford–
Bourne road, about
3 miles north of
Stamford, just
before the village of
Ryhall, turn left on
minor road
signposted Little
Casterton (about 1
mile). The Hall is on
the first road to the
right, just before
entering Little
Casterton

MAP REFERENCE:
130: 024104

Tolethorpe Hall

Nowadays Tolethorpe Hall is best known as the home of the Stamford Shakespeare Company which each year presents three plays during the summer months in an outdoor auditorium. The old manor house, partly medieval, rebuilt in the 1590s and 'restored' in 1867, has another claim to fame as the birthplace in 1550 of Robert Browne, one of the earliest 'congregationalists'. His radical views led to his arrest but through the intervention of his kinsman William Cecil, Lord Burghley, he was released and fled to Holland. His religious views mellowed with the passing of the years: his fiery temper did not. At the age of 80 he was sent to Northampton jail for an assault on a constable and it was there that he died in 1633.

OTHER PLACES
OF INTEREST

Tickencote (p. 111)
Exton (p. 41) and
Empingham (p. 40)
to the west;
Pickworth (p. 91)
and Clipsham
(p. 35) to the north-
west.

LITTLE DALBY

The Birthplace of Stilton Cheese?

Location: From the
A606 Melton
Mowbray–Oakham
road, about 4 miles
south-east of
Melton, turn right
on a minor road to
Little Dalby. After
about ¼ mile, take
the left fork, then
the right fork. The
footpath goes off to
the right about
400 yd up this road
MAP REFERENCE:
129: 776135

More than three hundred years after Stilton cheese arrived on the table, there are still acrimonious disputes about where this aristocrat of cheeses originated. Its name was taken from the Cambridgeshire village of Stilton but it certainly wasn't made there. All they did there was sell this strong-flavoured, smooth-on-the-tongue dairy product to travellers stopping off at the Bell Inn on the Great North Road. At various times, different authorities have credited Mary Beaumont of Kirby Bellars, Mrs Paulet of Wymondham, Elizabeth Scarbrow of Quenby Hall and Mrs Orton of Little Dalby Hall. When one discovers that the last two ladies are in fact one and the same, Little Dalby's rights to the title become stronger – Elizabeth Scarbrow was housekeeper at Quenby until she married and went to live at Little Dalby. Supporters of Quenby, however, assert that the cheese was already known there before Miss Scarbrow became Mrs Orton. And to confuse matters still further, the

Wymondham faction point out that their candidate, Mrs Paulet, was the daughter of an earlier housekeeper at Quenby and her brother-in-law was the landlord of the Bell Inn at Stilton!

Whether it's the true source of Stilton cheese or not, Little Dalby Hall is an attractive seventeenth-century manor house. It is not open to the public, but the Leicestershire Round long-distance footpath passes close by.

*OTHER PLACES
OF INTEREST*

*Burton Lazars
(p. 31) and Melton
Mowbray (p. 77) to
the north; Oakham
(p. 87) to the south-
east; Gaddesby
(p. 44) to the west.*

LOUGHBOROUGH

Drained Every Week of a Gallon of Water

One of the county's most bizarre gravestones is not to be found in consecrated ground but in Loughborough's Old Rectory Museum. In a blatant breach of doctor–patient confidentiality the tombstone records in great detail the medical history of Sarah Johnson, who died on 2 August 1819. Sarah suffered from ascites, or dropsy, the treatment for which was regular draining, or 'tapping', of the excess liquid trapped in her body. Her memorial includes a neat table giving the dates of the twenty-eight occasions on which Sarah was 'tapped', and the precise quantities of water collected from each operation. In the six years before she finally succumbed, her body was drained of a total of 310 gallons, 1 quart and 1 pint – on average, about one gallon a week.

Surprisingly, Sarah's tombstone is not unique. In St Peter's Church, Saxelbye, a similar memorial testifies that Esther Houghton was 'tap'd 21 times from August the 21st 1789 to April the 28th 1797. The Quantity of Water taken from her was 222 gallons, weighing 19 c [hundredweight], 2 qrs, 9 lbs'.

OTHER PLACES
OF INTEREST

Barrow upon Soar
(p. 8) to the east;
Mountsorrel (p. 82)
and Swithland
(p. 107) to the
south; Dishley
(p. 36) to the north-
west.

LOUGHBOROUGH

A War Memorial that Gives Recitals

Whoever decided that Loughborough's War Memorial should take the form of a Carillon Tower deserves full praise. As well as commemorating the dead of the First World War the Carillon provides one of the county's most pleasant free entertainments. During the summer months there are regular recitals with Queen's Park as an attractive setting for the audience. This isn't church tower bell-ringing – quite sophisticated melodies can be produced by the forty-seven differently sized bells. The smallest is just 7 in high and weighs 20 lb; the largest is 5 ft high and weighs more than 4 tons.

It was appropriate that the Carillon should be built here for Loughborough has been the centre of bell-making in England ever since 1839 when John Taylor moved to the town. His company made 'Great Paul', the mammoth bell with a mouth 9.5 ft wide and weighing 17 tons that was built in 1881 for St Paul's Cathedral. The huge bell was moved to London by road, taking ten days to get there, with the transport contractor leading the way on a tricycle. John Taylor's company is still flourishing and welcomes visitors, as does the Bell Foundry Museum next door in Freehold Street (tel. (01509) 233414).

OTHER PLACES
OF INTEREST

*Barrow upon Soar
(p. 8) to the east;
Mountsorrel (p. 82)
and Swithland
(p. 107) to the
south; Dishley (p.
36) to the north-
west.*

LUTTERWORTH

*Location: St Mary's
Church is in the
centre of
Lutterworth at the
junction of the
A427 and A426.
The obelisk stands
just outside*
MAP REFERENCE:
140: 544846

'The Morning Star of the Reformation'

By the time John Wycliffe became the Rector of Lutterworth in 1374 he was already well known for his radical criticisms of ecclesiastical abuses and his insistence that every man had the right to study the scriptures for himself. His translation of the Bible into English was widely disseminated by his followers, derisively known as 'Lollards' from a Dutch word for 'mumblers'. Pope Gregory XI denounced Wycliffe in 1377 but he was saved by the protection of John of Gaunt. Wycliffe died of a heart attack while celebrating Mass in Lutterworth church in December 1384 but the Lollard movement continued to incense church authorities. Thirty years after the death of the 'morning star of the Reformation', the Council of Constance pronounced heretical forty-five articles from his writings and ordered that his bones should be dug up, burned and the ashes thrown into the River Swift. This sentence was executed in 1428 and gave fresh vigour to the cult that preserved various 'relics' of his tenure as rector here. It was an ironic development for a man who had fought against the veneration of such spurious objects. Wycliffe's connection with Lutterworth is recalled by a fine marble tableau by the celebrated sculptor Richard Westmacott in St Mary's Church, and the obelisk outside.

*OTHER PLACES
OF INTEREST*

*Bitteswell (p. 19) to
the north; Stanford
Hall (p. 100) and
South Kilworth
(p. 98) to the south-
west; Claybrooke
Magna (p. 34) to
the north-west.*

LYDDINGTON

The Bishop's Banqueting Hall

Location: From the
A6003, about 2
miles south of
Uppingham, turn
left on an
unclassified road for
about 1 mile to
Lyddington
MAP REFERENCE:
141: 877971

One of the finest examples of Tudor domestic architecture, the Bede House in Lyddington was originally one of the Bishop of Lincoln's palaces, built when what is now a somnolent village was one of the administrative centres for his Diocese. Bishops had maintained a residence here for centuries but the present building dates back to the late 1400s. Its most glorious feature is a superb Banqueting Hall with a ceiling of panelled oak and richly carved tracery 'fit to grace a royal palace', and glorious heraldic windows of fifteenth-century stained glass. In the gardens is a delightful octagonal stone summer-house and just outside the grounds lie the fish ponds that used to supply the bishop's kitchen.

Lyddington's former importance as an ecclesiastical centre is reflected in the size of St Andrew's Church – much larger than you would expect for such a simple village. Its dimensions are perhaps the reason why, when the walls were built in the fourteenth-century, earthenware jars were enclosed in the fabric as a primitive form of amplification. You can still see the holes high up on the chancel walls.

*OTHER PLACES
OF INTEREST*

*Uppingham (p. 114)
to the north; Seaton
(p. 95) to the east;
Rockingham Castle
(Northants) to the
south.*

MARKET HARBOROUGH

Location: The Old
Grammar School is
on the A427 in the
centre of Market
Harborough
MAP REFERENCE:
141: 733872

A School on Stilts

One of the most striking small buildings in the county, the Old Grammar School was built in 1614 with two purposes in mind. The ground floor was 'to keepe the market people drye in time of fowle weather', for this is where the weekly butter market was held. The upper floor, supported on sturdy oak pillars, provided the classrooms for the school founded by Robert Smyth, a native of the town who had made his fortune in Elizabethan London. In his will he left an endowment of £40 a year for the upkeep of the school along with a stipulation that Biblical quotations should be painted along the outside walls. They're still there, still in good repair, as are the ornamental bargeboards and the pargetting (decorative plaster) which were added in 1869.

OTHER PLACES
OF INTEREST

Church Langton
(p. 33) to the north;
Hallaton (p. 48) and
Medbourne (p. 75)
to the north-east;
Foxton (p. 43) to
the north-west.

The school occupied these unorthodox premises for more than 250 years, finally moving out in 1892, but the unique building is still in constant use for meetings and exhibitions.

MARKET HARBOROUGH

At the Sign of the Three Swans

Location: The Hotel
is in the High Street,
just north of the
church
MAP REFERENCE:
141: 733872

T he stage coach era lasted for less than a century. It began with the advent of turnpike roads in the late eighteenth century, was boosted by MacAdam's invention of a new surfacing material, tarmacadam, and then annihilated by the railway revolution of the 1840s. Brief though it was, the heyday of this romantic (and uncomfortable) form of transport left behind a rich legacy in the form of the many coaching inns scattered across the country. As an important trading centre Market Harborough needed several of them and the Three Swans still retains the atmosphere of those

days. The long stabling yard is still there and so, too, is its superb wrought-iron sign showing three swans swimming through a filigree of delicate iron tracery. Made in the eighteenth century, it is a magnificent example of expert metalcraft. During the sixteenth century, the inn was known simply as The Swan – it's not known exactly when the other two were added.

*OTHER PLACES
OF INTEREST*

*Church Langton
(p. 33) to the north;
Hallaton (p. 48) and
Medbourne (p. 75)
to the north-east;
Foxton (p. 43) to
the north-west.*

MARKET OVERTON

Isaac Newton's Childhood Village

Location: From the
A1, about 11 miles
north of Stamford,
take the minor road
westwards into
South Witham. Just
before leaving this
village, turn left on
a minor road
signposted to
Thistleton and
Market Overton
MAP REFERENCE:
130: 886164

As a child in the 1640s and '50s, Isaac Newton would almost certainly have seen the stocks and whipping post on the village green at Market Overton in use. His mother, Harriet Ayscough, was born in the village but left when she married Isaac Newton the elder. The marriage was only six months old when her husband died. Isaac was born three months later, a tiny baby so small he 'could have been put into a quart mug'. Harriet soon remarried and Isaac was brought up by his grandmother in Market Overton. Thieves, drunkards and scolds would have served their time in the stocks; persistent offenders would have suffered a whipping or had part of an ear sliced off.

Isaac appears to have left Market Overton when he began attending Grantham Grammar School but he retained his association with the village – a sundial on one corner of the church tower is said to have been a gift from him in later years.

OTHER PLACES
OF INTEREST

Stretton (p. 105)
and Clipsham
(p. 35) to the east;
Exton (p. 41) and
Burley on the Hill
(p. 29) to the south;
Wymondham
(p. 118) to the
north-west.

MEDBOURNE

A Disastrous Wager

Location:
Medbourne is on
the B664, 10 miles
north-east of
Market Harborough
MAP REFERENCE:
141: 800929

The Nevill Arms Inn has that comfortable look of having been settled in place for ever, and there has indeed been an inn of that name here since medieval times. But this particular one was built in 1863 after its predecessor was burnt to the ground in somewhat unusual circumstances.

Towards the end of a boisterous evening's drinking at the inn, the village blacksmith was boasting that he could support the smithy's anvil on his chest while a horseshoe was being forged on it. Wagers were placed, four men lugged the anvil into place on the blacksmith's stomach and the forging began. Within minutes, stray sparks had set the hostelry on fire, and within a couple of hours the inn was completely gutted.

OTHER PLACES
OF INTEREST

Hallaton (p. 48) to
the north; Drayton
(p. 38) to the east;
Rockingham Castle,
(Northants) to the
south; and see
following page.

MEDBOURNE

A Bridge over the Meadow Brook

Location:
Medbourne is on
the B664, 10 miles
north-east of
Market Harborough
MAP REFERENCE:
141: 800931

An attractive village with many fine stone buildings, Medbourne has developed from a settlement in Roman times. Then there was a staging post here where the road from Leicester to Huntingdon crossed the River Welland. Medbourne takes its name, 'Meadow-brook', from the stream that runs through the village, skirting the Church of St Giles with its circular churchyard and cutting it off from the western part of the village. This hazard must have caused some difficulties for the devout and some time in the thirteenth century the lovely stone bridge, a mere 5 ft wide with four graceful arches, was erected over the stream. In summer, it's a good spot to watch kingfishers, swifts and herons darting above the shallow water.

OTHER PLACES
OF INTEREST

Hallaton (p. 48) to
the north; Drayton
(p. 38) to the east;
Rockingham Castle
(Northants) to the
south; and see
previous page.

MELTON MOWBRAY

A Demi-Cathedral

Location: St Mary's
Church is in the
centre of the town,
just off the Market
Place
MAP REFERENCE:
129: 753190

When the Diocese of Leicester was being created in 1926, there were many who advocated that Melton's St Mary's Church should become its cathedral. Built between 1170 and 1532 St Mary's is, in Pevsner's view, 'the stateliest and most impressive of all churches in Leicestershire', a demi-cathedral noted for its fine stained glass, unusual transepts and 100 ft tower. The superb clerestory contains more than fifteen thousand diamond-shaped pieces of clear glass, and each transept has a rare candelabra dating back to 1764.

Two famous names associated with the church were both devotees of Handel's *Messiah*. The eighteenth-century rector, Dr Ford, was obsessed by it and was constantly singing the arias. Attending one performance, he could not resist joining in the singing, causing a fellow member of the audience to object that he had not paid to hear Dr Ford sing. 'Then you have got that into the bargain,' the vicar rejoined. More recently, Sir Malcolm Sargent, who established his reputation with choral music, was organist and choirmaster at St Mary's from 1914 to 1924.

*OTHER PLACES
OF INTEREST*

*Burton Lazars
(p. 31) to the south-
east; Little Dalby
(p. 67) to the south;
Gaddesby
(p. 44) to the south-
west; Grimston
(p. 47) to the north-
west; and see
following pages.*

MELTON MOWBRAY

Anne of Cleves' House

*Location: Anne of
Cleves' House is on
Burton Street (the
A606) just south of
St Mary's Church*
MAP REFERENCE:
129: 753190

Anne of Cleves' House in Melton is one of severally identically named properties around the country, which were given by Henry VIII to his fourth wife as part of their divorce settlement in 1541. (Curiously, many of them are now restaurants or tea rooms.) Melton's Anne of Cleves' House was originally built in 1384 as a residence for chantry priests serving St Mary's Church close by. At the Dissolution of the Monasteries, it became a possession of the Crown for a short period before ownership was transferred to Anne. There is no evidence that she ever lived here and in recent years the house has had a succession of owners, most of whom have used it as a restaurant or tea room.

Just across the road are the Bede Houses (also known as the 'Maison Dieu') dated 1640 and founded by Robert Hudson, a townsman who had made a fortune as a London merchant. He endowed the houses for six elderly men and later, in the eighteenth century, room was made to accommodate six elderly women as well. They are still used as almshouses today.

*OTHER PLACES
OF INTEREST*

*Wymondham
(p. 118) to the east;
Burton Lazars
(p. 31) and Oakham
(p. 87) to the south-
east; Gaddesby
(p. 44) to the south-
west; and see
preceding and
following pages.*

MELTON MOWBRAY

A Misfortunate Beast

*Location: The
Carnegie Museum,
which also houses
the town's Tourist
Information Centre,
is on Thorpe End*
MAP REFERENCE:
129: 756192

In Melton Mowbray's Carnegie Museum a glass case contains an extraordinary freak of nature, a two-headed calf that was born at Braunston near Oakham around 1895. It was delivered by the local vet, Justus Littler, but survived only a few hours. Mr Littler had the body stuffed and cased and when he moved his practice to Melton Mowbray installed it in the waiting room of his surgery in Elgin Lodge. (Elgin Lodge, incidentally, was the home of the famous painter of hunting pictures, John Ferneley [*see* Thrussington, p. 110]. It was later destroyed by fire.)

During both World Wars, the aberrant creature was displayed in the Cattle Market as a peep-show to raise funds for the Red Cross and other charities. The Littler family's veterinary practice closed in the late 1970s and the exhibit was donated to the Carnegie Museum by Mr Littler's grand-daughter in 1981. Also on display in the Museum are six fine paintings by John Ferneley who spent much of his working life in Melton Mowbray.

Opening times. 10.00 a.m. – 5.00 p.m. (Monday – Saturday all year); 2.00 p.m. – 5.00 p.m. (Sundays in summer only). Museum: (01664) 469946; TIC: (01664) 480992.

*OTHER PLACES
OF INTEREST*

*Burton Lazars
(p. 31) to the south-
east; Little Dalby
(p. 67) to the south;
Gaddesby (p. 44)
to the south-west;
Grimston (p. 47) to
the north-west; and
see preceding pages.*

MELTON MOWBRAY

A Convenience Snack for Huntsmen

Location: Ye Olde
Pork Pie Shoppe is
on Nottingham
Street, just off the
Market Place
MAP REFERENCE:
129: 755192

The connection between Leicestershire's two great contributions to English cuisine, Stilton cheese and pork pies, is the watery serum called whey. A by-product of the process of making Stilton cheese, the whey was fed to pigs and produced a particularly succulent kind of pork. The history of Melton Mowbray's famous pork pies can be traced back to 1831 when Edward Adcock began baking them commercially in a small shop, now a café, next to the Fox Inn yard. The pies were especially popular with the hunting fraternity who found them a convenient form of nourishment.

Ye Olde Pork Pie Shoppe in Nottingham Street, north of the Market Place, has been making the pies since 1850. By appointment, you can watch the pies being hand-made. The pastry is raised by hand around a wooden mould – the bowed sides of the finished product are a sure indication that the pie has been made in the traditional way.

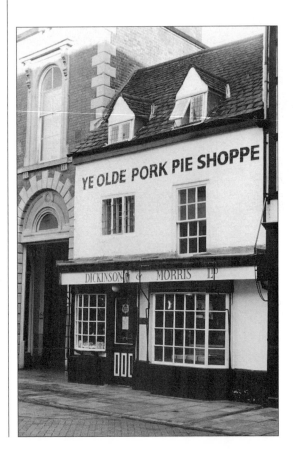

OTHER PLACES
OF INTEREST

Burton Lazars
(p. 31) to the south-
east; Little Dalby
(p. 67) to the south;
Gaddesby (p. 44) to
the south-west;
Grimston (p. 47) to
the north-west; and
see preceding pages.

MOIRA

A Little-Used Furnace

Location: Moira is
located on the
B5003
approximately 4
miles west of Ashby
de la Zouch.
MAP REFERENCE:
128: 315152

Moira Furnace is almost two hundred years old but seems to have been in operation for less than two. The Earl of Moira began building it in 1804 to smelt iron from the ore-bearing coal measures at nearby Ashby Woulds. But when the furnace was blown in during 1806 it remained in blast for just eleven months. The iron produced was of variable quality, there was little of it and the furnace consumed huge quantities of coke. The Earl tried again in 1810 but exactly the same difficulties arose again. After nine months the furnace was blown out, 'temporarily', and there is no evidence that it ever worked again.

Moira remains, however, one of the great monuments of the Industrial

Revolution and the forerunner of larger, more advanced furnaces. It is reckoned to be the best preserved in Europe, complete with a casting shed, engine house and now a museum. North-West Leicestershire District Council bought the site in 1982, restored the building, landscaped the surroundings and devised the 'Moira Furnace Trail' which guides visitors around the massive building and other locations associated with it.

For opening times contact Moira Furnace (01283) 224667.

*OTHER PLACES
OF INTEREST*

*Ashby de la Zouch
(p. 5) and Staunton
Harold (p. 102) to
the north-east;
Donington-le-Heath
(p. 37) to the east;
Appleby Magna
(p. 2) and Appleby
Parva (p. 3) to the
south.*

MOUNTSORREL

Location:
Mountsorrel is just
west of the A6, 5
miles south-east of
Loughborough
MAP REFERENCE:
129: 581149

A Passion for Red

Mountsorrel's elegant Butter Market, or Dome, lends distinction to an otherwise undistinguished little town ('a romantically named but singularly unattractive township,' a 1926 guidebook declared). Technically described as 'a neo-classical rotunda of eight Tuscan columns supporting a low-stepped dome surmounted by an urn', it was built in 1793 by the eccentric Lord of the Manor, Sir John Danvers. It replaced an equally elegant fifteenth-century market cross which Sir John removed to his own park at Swithland Hall nearby where it still stands.

Surprisingly, the Butter Market was not painted red. Almost everything else in Mountsorrel and Swithland that could be painted – doors, window shutters, gate posts – was covered in brilliant red, a colour for which Sir John had an insatiable passion. Even his clothes were predominantly red, set off by discreet touches of black: 'being a broad-set man his appearance was like that of the Knave of Spades'.

For more about the Danvers family, *see* Swithland, p. 107.

OTHER PLACES
OF INTEREST

Barrow upon Soar
(p. 8) to the north;
Wanlip (p. 115) and
Rothley (p. 94) to
the south; Swithland
(p. 107) and
Beaumanor Hall
(p. 10) to the west.

NEVILL HOLT

The Country Residence of the Cunards

83

Location: From the
B664, about 5 miles
south-west of
Uppingham, turn
left on an
unclassified road
signposted to Nevill
Holt and Drayton.
The Hall is about a
mile along this road
on the left
MAP REFERENCE:
141: 816938

Surrounded by rolling parkland, Neville Holt Hall sits on a hillside commanding panoramic views across the Welland Valley to Rockingham Castle. Dating back to the 1200s, the house was continually enlarged over the next four centuries and the complex includes the former parish church with its tall needle spire. In Victorian and Edwardian times the Hall was owned by the Cunard family who added the attractive lodge cottages and the superb set of iron gates guarding the entrance on the Medbourne road. The Hall is now a private school but the picturesque complex can be seen from the road and there are public footpaths crossing the grounds.

The Hall swamps the tiny hamlet which has a population of 115 but which enjoyed a brief spell as a spa in the mid-1700s.

OTHER PLACES
OF INTEREST

Uppingham (p. 114)
to the north-east;
Drayton (p. 38) to
the south;
Medbourne (p. 75)
to the west; Hallaton
(p. 48) to the north-
west.

NEWTON HARCOURT

Location: From the
A6 in Great Glen,
about 6 miles south-
east of Leicester,
turn right on an
unclassified road for
about 1.5 miles to
Newton Harcourt
MAP REFERENCE:
140: 640968

A Toy Church as a Memorial

Any tombstone commemorating a child has a special poignancy but Christopher Gardner's memorial in the graveyard of St Luke's, Newton Harcourt, is also believed to be unique in England. Christopher died at the age of 8 in 1924 and his grave is marked not by a conventional tombstone but by a miniature church. This sombre toy stands a little over 3 ft high, a three-dimensional model complete with spire, Norman doorway, battlements and even traceried windows. It is dedicated 'To the fragrant memory of Christopher Gardner'.

A less heart-rending memorial was left at St Luke's by Sir Henry Halford. Sitting at the window of the manor house one day, he noticed that despite the breezy weather the weather vane on the church tower was not veering with the wind. Seizing his gun, he began taking pot-shots at it to make it move. The gun-shot holes in the vane are still visible today.

OTHER PLACES
OF INTEREST

Church Langton
(p. 33) to the south-
east; Arnesby (p. 4)
and Shearsby (p. 96)
to the south-west;
Leicester (p. 54) to
the north-west.

NORMANTON

An Ill-Starred Village

85

Location: The Rutland Water Walk goes all the way round the lake. Parking is available at the Edith Weston entrance.

MAP REFERENCE: 141: 933063

The history of Normanton village has been singularly ill-starred. In the mid-eighteenth century it was a prosperous little community, with most of its work-force employed at Sir Gilbert Heathcote's grand mansion, Normanton Hall, or on his estate. In 1764, however, Sir Gilbert's son decided to enlarge the Park. The whole village was destroyed and all the villagers resettled at Empingham, about 2 miles away. Only the church and the Hall remained. The Hall was demolished in 1925 and then, in the 1970s, construction began on the largest man-made lake in Britain, Rutland Water. Some 30,000 gallons of water filled the valley, covering the sites of Hambleton village and the Hall. Only the building of a large embankment saved the church from being submerged by the rising waters.

Now it stands on a narrow promontory jutting out into the lake, the sole survivor of a once-thriving community.

Deconsecrated in 1970, the former church reopened in 1984 as the Normanton Church Water Museum and includes amongst its exhibits a well preserved Anglo-Saxon skeleton unearthed during excavations for the reservoir. For Museum opening times call (01780) 460321.

OTHER PLACES OF INTEREST

Empingham (p. 40) and Tickencote (p. 111) to the north-east; Wing (p. 117) to the south-west; Oakham (p. 87) to the north-west.

OADBY

'I Will Poach Till I Die'

Location: The
cemetery is near the
centre of Oadby,
beside the A5096
MAP REFERENCE:
140: 624004

One of the most engaging rogues of all time must be James Hawker, and one of the most enjoyable books ever written is his robust autobiography, *James Hawker's Journal*. James found his true vocation in life quite early – he was 18 years old when he poached his first bird. That was in 1844 and from then until his death in 1921 he honoured his declaration that 'I will poach till I die'. His book catalogues his many sins against the laws of the time but he was only caught once and on that charge, he indignantly claims, he was innocent – 'They knew me and seized the occasion to punish my earlier misdemeanours'.

In later life James happily combined a respectable day-time career as a parish councillor and member of the school board with a nocturnal pastime of depleting his aristocratic neighbours' land of their edible game. For sixty years his grave in Oadby Cemetery remained unmarked until the EMMA Theatre Company, which had performed a play about his life, erected a simple monument bearing as epitaph his defiant, and true, claim 'I will poach till I die'.

OTHER PLACES
OF INTEREST

Leicester (p. 54) to
the north; Billesdon
(p. 16) to the east;
Arnesby (p. 4) to
the south; Blaby
(p. 20) to the south-
west.

OAKHAM

Tom Thumb's House

Location: Tom Thumb's house is in the High Street about 400 yd east of the level crossing
MAP REFERENCE: 141: 858088

At the age of 9, Jeffery Hudson stood a mere 18 inches high. His father, who was if anything above average height, worked on the Duke of Buckingham's estate at Burley on the Hill just outside Oakham. The Duchess took a fancy to the minuscule lad, dressed him in costly silk and satin and kept him by her as a kind of mascot. When Charles I visited Burley, a large pie was served at dinner. When it was cut open, out jumped Jeffery, a *coup de théâtre* that so delighted Queen Henrietta Maria she must needs have the dwarf for herself.

The Queen had his portrait painted by Van Dyck and Jeffery accompanied her during her exile in Paris. Despite his diminutive size, he was extremely quarrelsome and on one occasion challenged Lord Crofts to a duel in which the latter was killed. Jeffery was banished, but while

travelling back to England he was captured by Turkish pirates and sold as a slave. Now 30 years old, he began to grow, eventually reaching a height of about 3 ft 6 in. Ransomed by the Duke of Buckingham, he returned to Oakham to the house in the High Street that still stands.

Part of the house is now a shop and therefore open to the public; the remainder is private.

OTHER PLACES OF INTEREST
Exton (p. 41) to the north-east; Wing (p. 117) to the south-east; Little Dalby (p. 67) to the west.

OAKHAM

*Location: The
Castle is signposted
from the Market
Square*
MAP REFERENCE:
141: 863 099

A Hagiography of Horseshoes

Of Oakham Castle only the twelfth-century Great Hall survives. It's one of the finest of its kind in the country but the sight that brings most visitors here is the remarkable collection of horseshoes displayed on its walls. For centuries, any peer of the realm passing through the town for the first time has been required to present a horseshoe to the castle. When this custom began isn't clear although one plausible story says that it began in the days of William the Conqueror when his farrier lived here. (The farrier's descendants, the Ferrers family, later built the Great Hall.) This unusual tax is still being imposed – amongst the hundreds of horseshoes of every size, some ornately gilded, others rusty, is one presented by Queen Elizabeth II.

*OTHER PLACES
OF INTEREST*

*Exton (p. 41) to the
north-east; Wing
(p. 117) to the south-
east; Uppingham
(p. 114) to the south;
Little Dalby (p. 67)
to the west, and see
previous page.*

OAKHAM

Rutland's Twin Schools

The tiny county of Rutland can boast two of the country's leading public schools, at Uppingham and Oakham. Both were founded by the same man, Robert Johnson, Archdeacon of Leicester, in the same year, 1584. The original school building at Uppingham still stands in the churchyard: so does the one at Oakham. Both are plain single-room buildings and both have inscriptions in Hebrew, Latin and Greek on the walls. Both schools were greatly enlarged in the nineteenth century, but while the school buildings at Uppingham dominate the little town, at Oakham they are spread across the town centre, part of them hidden away off the attractive market place where the ancient Butter Cross still provides shelter for the town stocks.

*OTHER PLACES
OF INTEREST*

*Exton (p. 41) to the
north-east; Wing
(p. 117) to the
south-east; Little
Dalby (p. 67) to the
west.*

Location:
Packington is on the
B5326 about 2
miles south of
Ashby de la Zouch
MAP REFERENCE:
128: 362147

PACKINGTON

The Village Lock-Up

The elegant little lock-up at Packington prompts two contradictory thoughts. One: criminal activity in the village during the eighteenth century couldn't have been all that rampant since there is hardly room inside the tiny, circular structure with its conical roof for more than one moderately sized malefactor. Two: very few other villages in the area felt the need to provide such accommodation at all, so perhaps Packington's mini-prison was more a demonstration of the villagers' dedication to the rule of law than a real deterrent to lawbreakers.

The lock-up stands in the garden of a private house in Ashby Road but is clearly visible from the pavement.

OTHER PLACES
OF INTEREST

Ashby de la Zouch
(p. 5) to the north;
Staunton Harold
(p. 102) to the
north; Breedon on
the Hill (p. 26) to
the north-east;
Moira (p. 81) to the
south-west.

PICKWORTH

Sweet Patty of the Vale

The sole surviving arch of Pickworth's medieval church would have been familiar to John Clare, surely one of the saddest figures amongst English poets. He knew Pickworth well, coming here as a young man and finding work on a nearby farm. Over the course of a year, he managed to save £1 from his meagre wages in order to publish a prospectus of his poems. The poems were eventually published but did not sell. Poverty, poor health and incipient madness stalked him throughout his life. His happiest years may well have been spent at Pickworth for it was near here that he met the 18-year-old Patty Turner, immortalized in one of his most charming poems:

> And I would go to Patty's cot,
> And Patty came to me,
> Each knew the other's every thought
> Under the hawthorn tree.
> And I'll be true for Patty's sake
> And she'll be true for mine,
> And I this little ballad make
> To be her Valentine.

They married soon afterwards and eventually had seven children but Clare was working beyond his strength and gradually his habitual melancholy deteriorated into madness. He spent the last twenty-seven years of his life in asylums. His youngest son went to see him once; Patty could never bring herself to visit.

*Location:
Pickworth is on an
unclassified road
about 6 miles north-
north-west of
Stamford. It is
reached most easily
by taking the B1081
from Stamford to
Great Casterton
(4 miles north-
west), at the
crossroads take the
signposted road due
north to Pickworth
(5 miles). At
Pickworth, turn left
at the crossroads
and the arch is
about
400 yd along this
road on the right*
MAP REFERENCE:

*OTHER PLACES
OF INTEREST*
*Empingham (p. 40)
and Tickencote
(p. 111) to the
south-west;
Clipsham (p. 35)
and Stretton
(p. 105) to the
north-west.*

PLUNGAR

*Location: Plungar is
on an unclassified
road, signposted
south from the A52
Nottingham–
Grantham road 2
miles east of
Bingham. The
tombstone stands
against the wall of
the porch*
MAP REFERENCE:
129: 769341

An Apprentice's Tombstone?

It must be one of the most incompetently carved gravestones ever to stand in a churchyard. Andrew Guy's wife Anne died on 8 December 1729 and the memorial slab he commissioned in her memory must have been a sore disappointment. His own name, for example, in the line ANNE, YE WIFE OF ANDREW starts boldly enough: ANDR but then reaches the edge of the stone, the EW having to be scrunched in above the R. Things had started going wrong at the very top of the inscription: BLESSED ARE THE DEAD WHO DIE IN THE LORD – 'ye' and 'Lord' have been compressed to a Y with a tiny 'e' above it (not that unusual) and 'L' with a minuscule 'd' above (unusual to the point of being sacrilegious).

The mason, an apprentice perhaps, had a similar problem with the first line of the memorial verse at the base of the stone. PALE DEATH WILL HARDLY FIND ANO it says, with the concluding syllable THER added with a flourish on the line above. A dense growth of ivy around the lower part of the stone obscures any other of the mason's misjudgements.

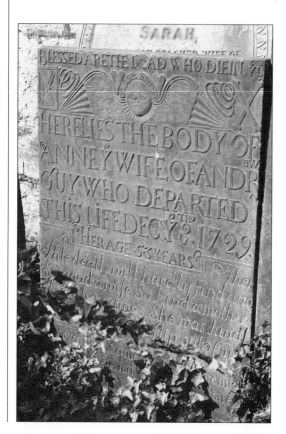

*OTHER PLACES
OF INTEREST*

*Bottesford (p. 21) to
the north-east;
Belvoir Castle
(p. 14) to the east;
Melton Mowbray
(p. 77) to the south.*

REARSBY

'£1 11s 0½d *Out of Pockett*'

Location: Rearsby is
just off the A607,
10 miles south-west
of Melton Mowbray
MAP REFERENCE:
129: 652146

Accheting to legend, the lovely old bridge in Rearsby was built by six men in just nine days during the summer of 1714. There had been trouble with the bridge two years earlier when the village constable, Robert Harrison, recorded a payment of eight pence 'for a plank laying down below the brigg, 2 stumps and 2 pinns' plus two pence for 'one day's work mending the brigg'.

When the bridge was completely rebuilt Harrison kept meticulous accounts. The total cost was £11 2s 2d (£11 11p) with the largest expense – £2 12s 6d – being 21 quarters of lime, the smallest a payment of 5d (2p) 'to George Skillington for Nailes'. The bridge was paid for by a levy on rate-payers of 8d in the pound but according to Harrison he ended up '£1 11s 0½d out of Pockett'. A small consolation must have been the inscription on the sixth arch of his initials, RH, alongside the date, 1714.

OTHER PLACES
OF INTEREST

*Thrussington
(p. 110) and
Brooksby (p. 27) to
the north; Gaddesby
(p. 44) to the east.*

ROTHLEY

The Soke of Rothley

Rothley Court Hotel must be unique amongst hotels in having its own medieval chapel. It was built in the thirteenth century as a preceptory of the Knights Templar and for centuries the house here was known as Rothley Temple. Crusader knights dedicated to recovering the Temple in Jerusalem, the order enjoyed considerable powers in civil and ecclesiastical matters in the Soke (or administrative district) of Rothley. Their emblem, a red cross on a white background, figures prominently on flags and plaques around the hotel. When the manor was bought by the Babington family in Tudor times, they also acquired the Knights Templar's anomalous powers, rights which they continued to exercise until the Reform Act of 1832.

For historians, Rothley Temple is something of a shrine. In 1800 the historian and poet Thomas Macaulay was born here and, when he was later elevated to the peerage, assumed the title Baron Macaulay of Rothley. Another famous historian, Macaulay's nephew Sir George Trevelyan, was also born at Rothley, in 1838.

Rothley Church is well worth seeking out. There are many monuments to the Babington family, an incised slab recording the death of Bartholomew Kyngston in 1486 and also giving the text of his will and, in the churchyard, a remarkable slate tomb of William Hunt (died 1794) with a carving showing the Last Judgement in Swithland churchyard.

SEATON

The Grandest Viaduct in the County

Location: The
viaduct crosses the
B672 from
Caldecott to
Morcott about
4 miles south-east of
Uppingham
MAP REFERENCE:
141: 914978

The broad valley of the River Welland to the east of Uppingham presented a major problem to the directors of the Midland Railway Company in the 1870s. They needed to get their track down into Northamptonshire and on to London but the only way to link the hills on each side was to build a massive viaduct. The cost would be enormous but they finally gritted their teeth and decided to go ahead.

The result was the longest viaduct in the county – a ¾ mile span requiring 82 brick arches 70 ft high, each of which cost a thousand pounds. Two thousand navvies, housed in a temporary settlement called Cyprus, laboured for four years until the viaduct was triumphantly opened in 1882. The line is still used for carrying freight but passenger services were withdrawn in 1966.

Beneath the northernmost arches of the viaduct run the abandoned trackbeds of the lines that used to run to Stamford and Uppingham.

OTHER PLACES
OF INTEREST

Rutland Water to
the north;
Lyddington (p. 71)
to the south-west;
Uppingham (p. 114)
to the north-west.

SHEARSBY

Location: Shearsby
is 10 miles south of
Leicester, just west
of the A50
MAP REFERENCE:
140: 624908

Spa Water that could Cure a Horse

D uring the early 1800s several places in the county, realizing that
they possessed a spring of disgusting-tasting water, tried to
emulate Harrogate's spectacular success as a spa town. Shearsby's
spring water wasn't particularly offensive – one of the reasons given for the
subsequent failure of the enterprise – but for several decades the village was
a popular resort for hypochondriacs. It wasn't cheap: a single bath cost
2s 6d (12½p), a course of nine, one guinea (£1 5p).

The spa's record of successful cures is not impressive: one villager who
claimed that his scurvy was much alleviated by bathing in the water, and
one General Pearson who sent a carriage and pair each day from his
residence 10 miles away to collect a barrel of Shearsby water. It wasn't for

him but for his favourite horse which was suffering from rheumatism. The
horse made a full recovery but the spa itself was in terminal decline. On its
site today stands the Bath Hotel, in its cellars the original baths where
patrons came to sample the 'efficacious waters'.

Also at Shearsby, in St Mary's churchyard, is a gravestone inscribed with
the laconic epitaph: 'In memory of William Weston who was unfortunately
catched in the windmill, and expired April 8th 1756 aged 36.'

OTHER PLACES
OF INTEREST

Lutterworth (p. 70)
and Bitteswell
(p. 19) to the south-
west; Arnesby (p. 4)
to the north.

SILEBY

A Revolving Sexton

Location: From the
A6, about 8 miles
south-east of
Loughborough, turn
left on an
unclassified road to
Sileby. The church is
at the T-junction as
you enter the village
MAP REFERENCE:
129: 600153

Two words in the inscription on Edward Baradell's gravestone in St Mary's churchyard have ensured that his epitaph is one of the most widely quoted in the county. In 1759, the year Edward died, the term 'revolving years' was the usual poetaster's cliché signifying 'passing time', but later generations have found the suggestion that the deceased sexton was some kind of spinning dervish irresistibly funny. The inscription on the elaborately chiselled stone reads in full:

> For fifty-two revolving years
> Devoutly he attended pray'rs
> With mellow voice and solemn knell
> He sung the psalms and toll'd the bell
> But cruel death spoiled his last stave
> And sent the sexton to his grave
> And his dear wife, loving and kind
> Stay'd but a little while behind.

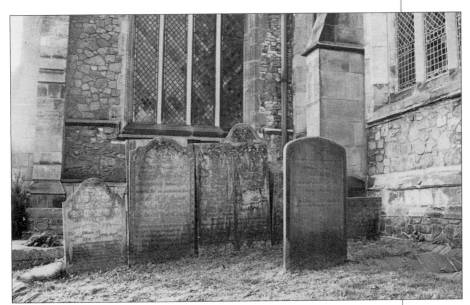

The graveyard here is notable also for the curious way in which old tombstones have been stacked up in files just like in a library.

OTHER PLACES
OF INTEREST

Barrow upon Soar
(p. 8) to the north-
west; Mountsorrel
(p. 82) to the west.

SOUTH KILWORTH

A Village Observatory

Location: South Kilworth is on the B5414 about 7 miles south-east of Lutterworth in the most southerly part of the county

MAP REFERENCE: 140: 605819

The Rector of South Kilworth between 1817 and 1847 was Dr William Pearson, a co-founder of the Royal Astronomical Society and author of many popular books on practical astronomy. At the rectory he covered one complete wing with a huge rotating dome for his astronomical studies and in 1834 built a state-of-the-art observatory just off the Rugby road, from which he computed the positions of more than five hundred stars. He brought with him to the village a finely crafted instrument which had originally been intended for the Observatory in St Petersburg, an intention frustrated by Napoleon's invasion of Russia. The unusual device became known as the South Kilworth Altitude and Azimuth Circle and is now in the Victoria & Albert Museum. The observatory he built has since been converted into a private house but can be seen from the road.

OTHER PLACES OF INTEREST

Stanford Hall (p. 100) to the south-west; Lutterworth (p. 70) and Bitteswell (p. 19) to the north-west.

SPROXTON

A Saxon Cross to Cross a Stream

The weatherbeaten Saxon cross that stands proudly in the churchyard at Sproxton has endured more in its thousand-year existence than just the assault of storm and frost. For many years it served as a rudimentary foot-bridge over a neighbouring stream. Then, late in the eighteenth century, a visiting antiquary noticed the intricate interlaced design carved along its length, and a chimerical creature, now known as the Anglian beast, climbing up its flank. The remarkable piece of Saxon workmanship was speedily removed to Sproxton churchyard but now looks sadly in need of a more protected location.

Location: From the A607 Melton Mowbray–Grantham road, turn south at Croxton Kerrial (about 10 miles north-east of Melton Mowbray). The church is about 4 miles south of Croxton Kerrial, just before entering the village of Sproxton

MAP REFERENCE: 130: 857249

OTHER PLACES OF INTEREST

Market Overton (p. 74) to the south-east; Wymondham (p. 118) to the south; Belvoir Castle (p. 14) and Bottesford (p. 21) to the north-west.

STANFORD HALL

Percy Pilcher's Fatal Flight

Location: Stanford
Hall is in the most
south-westerly
corner of the
county, off an
unclassified road
between Swinford
and Stanford on
Avon. It is widely
signposted.
MAP REFERENCE:
140: 587793

Towards the end of the nineteenth century, many experiments were made in the race to be the first person to build a viable flying machine. In the forefront of these pioneering aviators was Percy Pilcher. A friend of Adrian Verney-Cave, later 6th Lord Braye, Percy made several of his experiments with heavier-than-air flying machines in the grounds of Stanford Hall. In 1897, he had accomplished the first controlled flight in Britain but his attempt to better that record on 30 September 1899 was to end in disaster. His glider, *The Hawk*, was about 50 ft up in the air when a bamboo strut in the tail fractured, the machine turned on its back and crashed. Percy was dragged unconscious from the wreckage and died at the Hall two days later. A monument in the grounds pays tribute to this pioneer aviator and in the stable block there's a replica of *The Hawk* 'with its innumerable wires like the ribs of an umbrella'.

The Hall is open on Saturdays and Sundays from Easter Saturday to the end of September; on Bank Holiday Mondays and the Tuesdays following; from 2.00 p.m. – 6.00 p.m. (last admissions 5.30 p.m.).

OTHER PLACES
OF INTEREST

South Kilworth
(p. 98) to the north-
east; Lutterworth
(p. 70) and
Bitteswell (p. 19) to
the north-west.

STANFORD HALL

Let the Ferret take the Flex!

Set in meadows beside the River Avon, Stanford Hall presents a most satisfying prospect of a perfect English country house – pleasingly proportioned, dignified, serene. Flanked by avenues of noble trees and acres of landscaped gardens, the Queen Anne-style mansion is the residence of Lord Braye whose family came over with William the Conqueror and has lived here at Stanford since 1430.

One of the house's great charms is that so little has changed since it was completed in 1698 and when changes were necessary great pains were taken to preserve the fabric of the house. For example, when it was decided in the 1890s to install electric lighting, an ingenious means was found of cabling the rooms without removing the floorboards. A hole was made at each end of a room and the flex attached to a ferret. The ferret, thrust inside one hole, rapidly made its way to the other where a morsel of fresh rabbit was placed as a reward.

OTHER PLACES OF INTEREST

South Kilworth (p. 98) to the north-east; Lutterworth (p. 70) and Bitteswell (p. 19) to the north-west.

STAUNTON HAROLD

The Murderous Earl Ferrers

Location: Staunton
Harold Hall is
signposted off the
A453 about 4 miles
north-east of Ashby
de la Zouch and,
the most attractive
approach, from the
B587 about 4 miles
south of Melbourne.
MAP REFERENCE:
128: 380209

'For position, Staunton Harold, the house and chapel, are unsurpassed in the country – certainly as far as Englishness is concerned.' So wrote Nikolaus Pevsner in the 1950s and four decades later nothing has spoilt the lovely vista. But there's a dark and violent story associated with this graceful house for it was here, in January 1760, that the 4th Earl Ferrers shot and killed his steward, John Johnson. The Earl was notorious for his violent temper – his wife had been granted a divorce some months earlier on the ground of continual ill-treatment – and when Johnson refused to sell him a profitable farm his rage escalated into murder. Tried by his peers in the House of Lords, Earl Ferrers pleaded insanity (probably true) but he was found guilty and sentenced to hang.

For the execution, the earl donned his dazzling wedding suit of white satin with silver embroidery and generously tipped the executioner a purse of 5 guineas. (Unfortunately, he gave it to the assistant by mistake and an unseemly scuffle between him and the chief executioner ensued.) It was the last time a peer of the realm was executed in England, and the first time the trapdoor method of hanging was employed. That didn't go smoothly either. The height had been misjudged and when he dropped the Earl's feet touched the ground. The two executioners had to pull on his legs to despatch him but it was still four minutes before the Earl's agonies were over.

The Hall is now a Sue Ryder Home and the only part open to the public is the coffee shop but the church, grounds and the Stables Arts Complex may all be visited.

*OTHER PLACES
OF INTEREST*

*Castle Donington
(p. 32) to the north;
Belton (p. 13) and
Breedon on the Hill
(p. 26) to the east;
Ashby de la Zouch
(p. 5) to the south.*

STAUNTON HAROLD

'One of the Most Unspoiled Things in Leicestershire'

This National Trust church is surrounded by parkland in a beautiful lakeside setting. It is one of the few to have been built during the Commonwealth period, in 1653, and retains the original box pews, cushions and hangings, together with fine panelling and a painted ceiling. Its builder, Sir Robert Shirley, paid for its construction as an imaginative act of defiance against the austerities of a cheerless Puritan régime that condemned church towers as vanity and hymn-singing as frivolous.

Sir Robert heartily despised the Puritans' morose view of religion: they responded by repeatedly throwing him into the Tower of London (for plotting against the Commonwealth, they said). He died there while still a young man of 28 and his body was carried from London to be buried in a splendidly ostentatious tomb in the light and cheerful church he had built, a church which Pevsner regarded as 'one of the most unspoiled things in Leicestershire'.

OTHER PLACES OF INTEREST

Castle Donington (p. 32) to the north; Belton (p. 13) and Breedon on the Hill (p. 26) to the east; Ashby de la Zouch (p. 5) to the south.

STOKE GOLDING

Location: The
village is on an
unclassified road 3
miles north-east of
Hinckley
MAP REFERENCE:
140: 398973

A Penance for 'Gowging'

In past times, misbehaviour in church seems to have attracted some unusual punishments (like the finger pillory at Ashby de la Zouch, *see* p. 6), but Mrs Frith of Stoke Golding was probably the last to have been sentenced to perform a public penance after her disgraceful conduct in St Margaret's Church. As part of the church restoration in the 1840s, the privately owned high-sided pews had been removed and replaced by free, open seats. Mrs Frith, landlady of the village inn, had owned one of the pews and on her first visit to the church after its restoration found a man sitting in what she considered her own particular place. She attacked him – 'lugged him and gowged him' – with such vigour that she was summoned before the ecclesiastical court in Leicester charged with brawling in church.

Her penance was to stand at the church door, wrapped in a sheet and holding a candle, for three successive Sundays as the congregation arrived, 'a sentence duly carried out to the edification of the multitudes assembled to witness its execution'.

OTHER PLACES
OF INTEREST

Fenny Drayton
(p. 42) to the west;
Hinckley (p. 50) to
the south; Sutton
Cheney (p. 106) to
the north.

STRETTON

Legends of the Ram Jam Inn

105

Location: The Ram Jam Inn is located on the west side of the A1, about 9 miles north of Stamford
MAP REFERENCE: 130: 946161

According to Arthur Mee, the Ram Jam Inn on the Great North Road takes its name 'from a delectable drink sold to coach passengers in the 18th century'. It appears that the landlord, Charles Blake, had been to India and returned with a powerful concoction which he named Ram Jam. (A drink called 'Rambooze', made of wine, ale, eggs and sugar, has been recorded, but so far no mention of 'Ram Jam' has been found.) Proud of his fiery drink, Charles Blake placed boards over the front door advertising 'Fine Ram Jam' and 'The Ram Jam House'. Before long the name 'Ram Jam' had supplanted the hostelry's official title, The Winchilsea Arms.

A different explanation of the inn's unusual name is now generally discounted although it enjoyed a long currency. According to this version, a rascally traveller offered to show the landlady how to draw mild and bitter from the same barrel. Taking her down into the cellar, he drilled a hole in one side of a barrel and told her to RAM her thumb into it. Then he drilled a hole in the other side and asked her to JAM her thumb into that. Then he left, leaving behind a large unpaid bill.

OTHER PLACES OF INTEREST

Clipsham (p. 35) to the east; Empingham (p. 40) to the south; Exton (p. 41) and Greetham (p. 46) to the south-west.

SUTTON CHENEY

*Location: The
Centre is signposted
off the A5 between
Hinckley and
Atherstone, and off
the A447 between
Hinckley and Long
Eaton*
MAP REFERENCE:
140: 398999

King Dick's Well

On a warm and sunny August morning in 1485 the Middle Ages in England came to an abrupt end on open ground near the village of Sutton Cheney. After less than an hour's combat the last of the Plantagenet kings, Richard III, lay dead. His crown, recovered from a bush, was now borne by the first of the Tudors, Henry VII. Bosworth Field today is the 'Battlefield Visitor Centre and Country Park', providing an exceptionally informative guide to one of the three most significant battles in British history (Hastings, 1066, and the Battle of Britain, 1940, are reckoned to be the others). The Battlefield Trail at Bosworth guides visitors to King Dick's Well where Richard is said to have taken his last drink: the dumpy stone pyramid was not erected above it until many years later.

The Tudors showed scant respect for the vanquished Richard. His mother was refused permission to claim the body which was unceremoniously buried at the Grey Friars priory in Leicester. Half a century later, at the Dissolution of the Monasteries, it was disinterred, tossed into the River Soar and never seen again.

The Battlefield Visitor Centre is open weekdays 1p.m. – 5p.m.; weekdays and Bank Holiday Mondays 11a.m. – 6p.m.; and during July and August, 11a.m. – 5p.m. Senior Warden: David Hardwick, tel. (01455) 290429.

*OTHER PLACES
OF INTEREST*

*Fenny Drayton
(p. 42) and Stoke
Golding (p. 104) to
the south-west;
Elmesthorpe (p. 39)
to the south-east.*

SWITHLAND

The 'In and Out' Tomb

Location: Swithland
Church is on an
unclassified road
between Rothley
and Woodhouse
Eaves, about 2 miles
west of Rothley
MAP REFERENCE:
129: 555128

Until it was replaced by the cheaper and less colourful Welsh variety, Swithland slate was highly prized across the county for roofing and, especially, for gravestones. The churchyard at St Leonard's has a remarkable collection of them, the earliest dating back to 1673. Many are ingeniously shaped and engraved with ornate cursive inscriptions, the later ones in particular verging on the ostentatious. One of the grandest tombs in this style is a superbly ornamented, block-shaped sarcophagus placed half in and half out of the graveyard. This curious arrangement was to enable Sir Joseph Danvers, who died in 1753, to share the same tomb as his favourite dog, 'Bodyguard'. His pet, of course, could not be buried in consecrated ground: Sir Joseph lies on the sanctified side of the churchyard wall, his dog on the other.

Inside there are more notable monuments, including one erected by Sir John Danvers (son of Sir Joseph) six years before his death. This premature memorial created the problem of how to record his actual date of death, a puzzle that was solved by stating, at the beginning of the immensely long epitaph 'The body of Sir John Danvers, Bart. who departed this life about the eighteenth century . . .' Sir John only just validated the inscription by dying in 1796.

For more about the Danvers family, *see* Mountsorrel, p. 82.

OTHER PLACES
OF INTEREST
Rothley (p. 94) and
Mountsorrel (p. 82)
to the east; Bradgate
Park (p. 24) to the
south.

SWITHLAND

Location: Swithland
is on an unclassified
road between
Rothley and
Woodhouse Eaves,
about 2 miles west
of Rothley
MAP REFERENCE:
129: 551131

Gazebo or Lock-Up?

In the garden of No. 173 Main Street, Swithland, stands a small circular tower, two storeys high, with a pointed roof of Swithland slate. The tiny one-light windows are probably the reason why local people usually refer to this curious building as a lock-up. Architectural historians, however, point out that there are two more of these towers at opposite ends of the site of Old Swithland Hall. It is much more likely, in their view, that these were folly boundary towers or gazebos.

OTHER PLACES
OF INTEREST

Rothley (p. 94) and
Mountsorrel (p. 82)
to the east; Bradgate
Park (p. 24) to the
south.

Syston

A Nine Days' Wonder

Location: Syston is
just to the east of
the A46 Leicester
–Newark road,
about 6 miles north
of Leicester
MAP REFERENCE:
129: 623118

Close to the Fosse Way, on the northern edge of Syston village, an unpretentious bridge crosses a tributary stream of the River Wreake. It's neither beautiful nor elegant but when it was originally built in 1797 it was literally a 'nine days' wonder'. The bridge was constructed by a team of three bricklayers and six labourers, using 25,000 bricks and 150 tons of stone. Although no documentation has been found to establish how long it took to transform this huge amount of material into a bridge, there is an enduring tradition that the nine labourers completed the work in just nine days. The bridge was repaired in 1868 and again in 1938.

OTHER PLACES
OF INTEREST

Rearsby (p. 93) and
Thrussington
(p. 110) to the
north; Gaddesby
(p. 44) to the north-
east; Leicester
(p. 54) to the south;
Bradgate Park
(p .24) to the west

THRUSSINGTON

Location:
*Thrussington lies
just off the A607,
about 8 miles south-
west of Melton
Mowbray*
MAP REFERENCE:
129: 650158

'Animal Painter'

Leicestershire's most famous artist, John Ferneley, began his career by painting pictures on the sides of farm waggons being repaired by his father, a wheelwright. These early works came to the notice of the 5th Duke of Rutland who, in 1801, paid for the 18-year-old lad to study in London. His talent flowered and by the time he moved to Melton Mowbray in 1814 Ferneley was much in demand as a gifted painter of horses, hunting scenes and hunting people. The affluent hunting fraternity of Melton showered him with commissions (10 guineas for painting a horse; between 30 and 60 guineas for a group scene).

Several of his paintings can be seen at Melton's Carnegie Museum and there's a larger collection on display at Leicester's Museum and Art Gallery. When he died in 1860 he was buried in Thrussington churchyard, on his gravestone the succinct two-word epitaph: ANIMAL PAINTER. The inscription is now virtually illegible. If you follow the narrow lane near the green between No. 15 The Green, and No. 16 Blue Boar Cottage, you can still see the remains of his father's forge and workshops.

*OTHER PLACES
OF INTEREST*

*Brooksby (p. 27) to
the east; Gaddesby
(p. 44) to the south-
east; Rearsby (p. 93)
to the south.*

TICKENCOTE

Only at Tickencote and Canterbury Cathedral . . .

Location: From the
A1, about 5 miles
north of Stamford
(Lincs), take the
minor road towards
Empingham. After
1.2 miles turn left at
the crossroads to
Tickencote, about
2 miles
MAP REFERENCE:
129: 990090

The exterior of St Peter's Church, rebuilt in 1791, presents a curious mishmash of pseudo-Norman architecture, but inside you'll find the genuine twelfth-century article. Only in the choir of Canterbury Cathedral is there anything to compare with the dramatic sexpartite vaulting over the chancel, a feature so rare in Norman building that Tickencote and Canterbury are the only examples in this country.

Equally extraordinary is the chancel arch, a mighty six-layered frame to the tiny nave beyond. Built around 1140, each of the six arches is carved with a different design – square-cut foliage, chevrons, double zigzags, beak-head ornament or just plain round mouldings. Its third feature is the most elaborate, grotesque figures alternating with foliage and the kind of carvings beloved by Norman masons – muzzled bears, crowned heads looking different ways (perhaps a reference to King Stephen and Queen Maud) and satiric images like that of a fox holding a monk's head between his teeth.

As well as these masterworks of Norman architecture, St Peter's Church contains a remarkably fine thirteenth-century font and an unusual wooden effigy, life-size, of a fourteenth-century knight. And, running the whole length of the chancel above the sexpartite vaulting, is the original Priest's Chamber. During the eighteenth-century restoration work the steps leading to it were removed and it can now only be reached through the ceiling of the vestry.

OTHER PLACES
OF INTEREST
Clipsham (p. 35)
and Stretton
(p. 105) to the
north; Little
Casterton (p. 66) to
the east;
Empingham (p. 40)
to the west; Exton
(p. 41) to the north-
west.

TWYCROSS

Location: On the
A444 between
Nuneaton and
Burton on Trent
MAP REFERENCE:
140: 339049

The Best French Stained Glass in England

A modest village church in west Leicestershire is, according to Pevsner, 'worth a pilgrimage of many miles' for it contains one of the county's most surprising treasures. The glorious east window of St James's, Twycross, is agleam with some of the most superlative stained glass in Europe, triumphs of medieval artistry that originally graced the Cathedral of St Denis and the Sainte-Chapelle in Paris. The glass was removed for safety during the French Revolution and bought by a wealthy Englishman who smuggled it out of the country and later presented it to William IV. The King in turn gave some of it to Earl Howe of Gopsall Park near Twycross and the richly coloured pieces, dating from about 1145, were installed in the Earl's local church.

During the Second World War, the glass was again removed for safe keeping. Then, when it had been replaced once more, the French Government tried, but failed, to buy the pieces back. These medieval masterpieces remain in place as one of Leicestershire's rarest treasures.

OTHER PLACES
OF INTEREST

Appleby Magna
(p. 2) and Appleby
Parva (p. 3) to the
north; Fenny
Drayton (p. 42) to
the south.

ULVERSCROFT

A Chimney Through the Rock

Location: From Exit
22 of the M1, take
the A50 towards
Leicester. Take the
first exit, the B587,
and almost
immediately turn
right on an
unclassified road. At
the first crossroads,
turn right. The
house is on the left
about 300 yd along
this road. The
houses are privately
owned

MAP REFERENCE:
129: 498116

Stoneywell Cottage looks as if it belongs in a children's story book – one can imagine Little Red Riding Hood's grandmother living there. Its large roof dips and rises as though wearied by the weight of centuries but in fact the house was built in 1899 by the distinguished Leicester-born architect Ernest Gimson (1864–1919) for his elder brother and has remained in the Gimson family to this day.

Stoneywell Cottage fits snugly into the terrain – so snugly that its chimney is actually hollowed out from the natural rock. Stoneywell is one of three cottages in Ulverscroft that Ernest built for members of his

family. The other two, Lea Cottage and Rockyfield, show unmistakable signs of the same architectural provenance with extensive roofs and gables placed at odd angles to each other. Together, they make a charming ensemble.

*OTHER PLACES
OF INTEREST*

Ruins of thirteenth-
century Ulverscroft
Priory (also private)
just outside the
village; Swithland
(p. 107) to the
north-east; Bradgate
Park (p. 24) to the
south-east.

UPPINGHAM

Location: The old school stands in the churchyard of St Peter and St Paul in the centre of the town.

MAP REFERENCE: 141: 866997

'Train Up a Child in the Way He Should Go'

O ther places are dominated by castles or cathedrals: in Uppingham it's the impressive buildings of its famous public school that give the little town its special character. The school was founded in 1584 by Robert Johnson, Archdeacon of Leicester, who for good measure also established Rutland's other celebrated school at Oakham in the same year. For more than two and a half centuries Uppingham School was just one of many such small grammar schools, giving rigorous instruction in classical languages to a couple of dozen local children. Then, in 1853, the Revd Edward Thring was appointed headmaster. During his thirty-four year tenure the sleepy little school was transformed.

The original school building near the churchyard, with its trilingual inscriptions around the walls in Latin, Greek and Hebrew ('Train up a child in the way he should go'), was abandoned. In its place rose a magnificent complex of neo-Gothic buildings: not just the traditional classrooms and a (splendid) chapel, but also a laboratory, workshops, museum, gymnasium and the most extensive school playing fields in the country. When the Revd Thring retired in 1897 he could look back with satisfaction on the creation of one of the country's most successful public schools (both academically and financially).

The old school is open on Saturday afternoons from 2.15 p.m. during June, July and August. At other times, Uppingham School Tours (01572) 822672 conducts tours of both the old and the present schools for pre-booked groups.

OTHER PLACES OF INTEREST

Braunston (p. 25) and Oakham (p. 87) to the north; Seaton (p. 95) to the south-east; Hallaton (p. 48) and Medbourne (p. 75) to the south-west; Launde (p. 53) to the west.

WANLIP

Two Interesting Memorials

Location: From the
A6 1 mile south of
Rothley, turn left on
an unclassified road
for about 1 mile to
Wanlip
MAP REFERENCE:
129: 603111

The English language nowadays is so predominant around the world that it's hard to believe that until well into the sixteenth century it was regarded (even by the English) as an 'uncouth tongue', incapable of matching the subtleties of the still-universal language of Latin. So Sir Thomas Walsh was something of a pioneer when he chose the vernacular for his brass memorial in the Church of Our Lady and St Nicholas at Wanlip. This is one of the finest brasses and its date, 1393, makes it the earliest one known to have its inscription in English.

The well-preserved memorial shows Sir Thomas in armour standing on a lion, his wife by his side with two dogs peeking out from her robe. The inscription reads, in part: '*Here lyes Thomas Walsh, knyght, lorde of Anlep [Wanlip] and dame Katine his wyfe, whiche in yer tyme made the kirke of Anlep and halud [hallowed] the kirkyerd first in worchip of God, and of oure Lady and seynt Nicholas.*'

In the churchyard stands the Egyptian-styled monument to the memory of a former slave: '*Rasselas Morjan, who was born at Macadi, on the confines of Abyssinia, and died at Wanlip Hall, August 25th, 1839. Rescued from a state of slavery in this life and enabled by God's grace to become a member of His church*'.

The young African had been baptized at Wanlip and was popular among his fellow-servants at Wanlip Hall, but we know very little more. It's possible that Rasselas had been rescued by the Babingtons of Rothley Temple a few miles away since they were prominent opponents of the slave trade. It seems appropriate that Rasselas should have come to Wanlip where the anti-slavery campaigner William Wilberforce lived for several years. Wilberforce died in 1833 so it's unlikely that the great reformer and the liberated slave ever met.

OTHER PLACES
OF INTEREST

Rothley (p. 94) to
the north; Leicester
(p. 54) to the south.

WIGSTON

Location: Wigston
cemetery is on the
west side of the
A50, about 1.5 mile
south of Wigston
town centre
MAP REFERENCE:
140: 609979

The Grave of Nellie Dean

Her grave lies at the furthest boundary of Wigston's sprawling cemetery, butted up against the iron railings that divide it from the school playing fields beyond. It's almost as if this memorial to one of the most popular performers in Edwardian vaudeville were not really welcome here. Her real name was Gertrude Ross, but as Gertie Gitana she entranced music-hall patrons with her heart-breaking renditions of sentimental songs such as 'Silver Bell', 'Kitty Dear' and her bring-down-the-house, bring-out-the-handkerchiefs number, 'Nellie Dean'. A winged angel drops its eyes to a square plinth at its feet inscribed with a verse from that plaintive song:

> There's an old mill by the stream, Nellie Dean,
> Where we used to sit and dream, Nellie Dean,
> And the waters as they flow,
> Seem to murmur sweet and low,
> You're my heart's desire, I love you, Nellie Dean.

As a postscript, her husband, Wigston-born impresario Don Ross has added the words:

> The Curtain's down, the show is done,
> And we are home again dear one.

OTHER PLACES
OF INTEREST

Leicester (p. 54) to
the north; Oadby
(p. 86) to the
north-east; Newton
Harcourt (p. 84) to
the south-east;
Arnesby (p. 4) and
Shearsby (p. 96) to
the south.

WING

'Quaint Mazes in the Wanton Green'

Location: Wing is
signposted off the
A6003 about
6 miles south of
Oakham, and off
the A47 about
2 miles east of
Uppingham
MAP REFERENCE:
129: 895028

The design of the turf maze at Wing is identical to the mosaic patterns in the floors of Chartres Cathedral and other French cathedrals. An old tradition asserts that penitents were required to crawl around the maze on their knees, stopping at various points to say prayers. But mazes have a history that long pre-dates Christian times, going back at least as far as the Minoan civilization of Crete. Reaching the centre of the maze represented death: finding your way back out, resurrection. The Celtic tribes perceived a magical element in the spiral form and it was they who brought mazes to Britain and in medieval times there were hundreds of turf mazes across the country.

By Shakespeare's time most had fallen into disuse. In *A Midsummer Night's Dream* he wrote – 'And the quaint mazes in the wanton green, / For lack of tread, are undistinguishable'. But the people of Wing perhaps possessed a mystical streak. As late as 1846 the *Leicester and Rutland Directory* noted 'An ancient Maze, in which the rustics run at the parish feast'. Around that time the village was also famous as the home of the 'Wise Woman of Wing', Amelia Woodcock, a herbalist whose medicines were so effective they were still being sold a century after her death in 1850 at Boots the chemists in Uppingham.

OTHER PLACES
OF INTEREST

Normanton (p. 85)
to the north-east;
Uppingham (p. 114)
and Lyddington
(p. 71) to the south-
west; Oakham
(p. 87) to the north-
west.

WYMONDHAM

A Noble Windmill

Location: *From the B676 Melton Mowbray–Colsterworth road, turn right at Garthorpe, signposted to Wymondham. After about 2 miles you will come to the windmill on your right just before you enter the village*

MAP REFERENCE: 130: 850193

Wymondham's broad main street bears witness to the village's former status as a market town with its own Grammar School, one of the many benefactions of the Sedley family. Crowning the hill just to the north of this attractive village stands a noble nineteenth-century windmill, the only one in the county that is regularly open to visitors. Inside the five-storey ironstone tower all the venerable machinery is still intact and the six sails, removed in 1922 after being damaged in a gale, are being lovingly restored. The mill out-buildings have been converted into small craft shops and a tea-room.

For many years, Wymondham was one of the major producers of Stilton cheese and there are many who believe that the cheese originated here. According to their version, around 1730 a Mrs Paulet of Wymondham was the first to make the succulent, aromatic cheese. Its fame spread and soon she was supplying the landlord of the Bell Inn, a hostelry on the Great North Road at a village called Stilton. (But see the entry for Little Dalby, p. 67, for an alternative claim.)

OTHER PLACES OF INTEREST

Sproxton (p. 99) to the north; Greetham (p. 46) to the south-east; Burley on the Hill (p. 29) to the south; Melton Mowbray (p. 77) to the west.

WYMONDHAM

A Defiant Epitaph

Location: From the
B676 Melton
Mowbray–
Colsterworth road,
turn right just
before Saxby,
signposted to
Wymondham. The
church is down a
lane opposite the
post office
MAP REFERENCE:
130: 852187

The vogue for displaying rhyming verses on gravestones flourished in the late eighteenth and early nineteenth centuries. At Wymondham this new fashion was embraced with enthusiasm and a whole corner of the graveyard is filled with lolling tombstones inscribed with crumbling testimonies to the departed.

The most popular of these is undoubtedly the defiant epitaph Samuel Pears penned for himself. A rag and bone man, he died on 3 March 1809 at the age of 91. At that time such a dubious trade barely merited Christian burial, but Samuel's epitaph is far from apologetic:

> I in my time did gather rags
> And many a time I filled my bags
> Al-tho it was a ragged trade
> My rags are sold and debts are paid,
> Therefore go on don't waste your time
> On bad biography and bitter rhyme
> For what I am this cumbrous clay assures
> And what I was is no affair of yours.

OTHER PLACES
OF INTEREST

Sproxton (p. 99) to
the north; Greetham
(p. 46) to the south-
east; Burley on the
Hill (p. 29) to the
south; Melton
Mowbray (p. 77) to
the west.

BIBLIOGRAPHY

Bailey, Brian, *Portrait of Leicestershire* (Robert Hale, 1977)

Bennett, J.D, *Who was Who in Leicestershire, 1500–1970* (Book House, 1975)

Billson, C.J., *Vestiges of Paganism in Leicestershire* (1911. Reprinted by Heart of Albion Press, 1994)

Firth, J.B., *Highways and Byways of Leicestershire* (Macmillan, 1926)

Hawker, James, *A Victorian Poacher* (Oxford University Press, 1961, paperback 1978)

Hopewell, Jeffrey, *Shire Guide to Leicestershire* (Shire Publications, 1989)

Hoskins, W.G., *Shell Guide to Leicestershire* (Faber & Faber, 1970)

——, *Shell Guide to Rutland* (Faber & Faber, 1963)

Lee, Joyce, *Who's Buried Where in Leicestershire* (Leicestershire Libraries, 1991)

Mee, Arthur, *The King's England – Leicestershire & Rutland* (Hodder & Stoughton, 1966)

Newman, Bernard, *Portrait of the Shires* (Hale, 1968)

Nichols, John, *The History & Antiquities of the County of Leicester* (1795–1815; Reprinted by SR Publications, 1971)

Palmer, Roy, *The Folklore of Leicestershire & Rutland* (Sycamore Press, 1985)

Pevsner, Nikolaus, *The Buildings of England, Leicestershire & Rutland* (Penguin, 1984)

Victoria History of the County of Leicester